INSANELY PRACTICAL LEADERSHIP

Copyright © 2024 by Stephen Blandino

Published by AVAIL

All rights reserved. No portion of this book may be reproduced, stored in a retrieval system, or transmitted in any form or by any means—electronic, mechanical, photocopy, recording, scanning, or other—except for brief quotations in critical reviews or articles, without prior written permission of the author.

Unless otherwise specified, all Scripture quotations are taken from the Holy Bible, New Living Translation, copyright © 1996, 2004, 2015 by Tyndale House Foundation. Used by permission of Tyndale House Publishers, Inc., Carol Stream, Illinois 60188. All rights reserved. | Scripture quotations marked ESV are from The ESV® Bible (The Holy Bible, English Standard Version®), copyright © 2001 by Crossway, a publishing ministry of Good News Publishers. Used by permission. All rights reserved. | Scripture quotations marked MSG are taken from THE MESSAGE, copyright © 1993, 1994, 1995, 1996, 2000, 2001, 2002 by Eugene H. Peterson. Used by permission of NavPress. All rights reserved. Represented by Tyndale House Publishers, Inc. | Scripture quotations marked NCV are taken from the New Century Version®. Copyright © 2005 by Thomas Nelson. Used by permission. All rights reserved. | Scripture quotations marked NIV are taken from the Holy Bible, New International Version®, NIV®. Copyright © 1973, 1978, 1984, 2011 by Biblica, Inc.™ Used by permission of Zondervan. All rights reserved worldwide. www.zondervan.com. The "NIV" and "New International Version" are trademarks registered in the United States Patent and Trademark Office by Biblica, Inc.™ |

For foreign and subsidiary rights, contact the author.

Cover design by: Sara Young
Cover photo by: Andrew van Tilborgh

ISBN: 978-1-964794-10-5   1 2 3 4 5 6 7 8 9 10

Printed in the United States of America

INSANELY PRACTICAL LEADERSHIP

12 NO-NONSENSE KEYS TO MASTER THE ART OF LEADING YOURSELF AND OTHERS

STEPHEN BLANDINO

AVAIL

PRAISE FOR
INSANELY PRACTICAL LEADERSHIP

Leadership starts with self-leadership, and Stephen Blandino models this so well. If you don't consider yourself a natural leader, take heart. Stephen shows us how to become a "learned leader." No matter where you are in your leadership journey, this book will help you take the next step.

—*Mark Batterson*
NYT bestselling author of The Circle Maker

All leaders will love my friend Stephen Blandino's book *Insanely Practical Leadership*. The book helps us understand the differences between a natural and a learned leader and how to appreciate, grow, and even leverage our leadership. The practicality of the book is refreshing, and you'll find yourself sharing the book and its insights with leaders you love.

—*Sam Chand*
Leadership consultant and author of VOICES

Insanely Practical Leadership lives up to its name. Not only does Stephen Blandino provide you with an extraordinarily practical game plan to lead yourself and others, but he also equips you with a powerful tool to train your staff and develop your leaders.

—*Scott Wilson*
Founder of Ready Set Grow
Author of Impact: Releasing the Power of Influence

I wholeheartedly endorse *Insanely Practical Leadership* by Stephen Blandino. This book brilliantly combines a structured approach with clear targets, a well-defined roadmap, and built-in accountability, ensuring that every step in the process is both purposeful and Spirit-led. It's an incredibly practical and impactful guide that equips you with the tools for personal growth and for leading others effectively.

—*Gerad Strong*
Director of Leadership and Training
Church Multiplication Network

Insanely Practical Leadership by Stephen Blandino is one of the most refreshingly honest, authentic, and actionable leadership books I've ever read. Drawing from years of personal experience, successes and failures, and a wealth of the best research on leadership, Stephen offers a clear, concise, and comprehensive leadership tool to grow yourself and the people you lead. I will use this book for formational development of seasoned leaders and also for foundational discipleship for emerging leaders.

—*Heather Zempel*
Dream Collective Executive Director
National Community Church

Stephen Blandino's take on *Insanely Practical Leadership* is just what a leader needs to move from knowing leadership to actually doing leadership. With clear, actionable insights, Stephen provides a straightforward roadmap for mastering the art of leading yourself and others.

—*Jeremy Yancey*
Lead Pastor, Timber Creek Church
Author of Good In Tension

As someone who doesn't feel like a natural leader, *Insanely Practical Leadership* gave me handles to grow and become the person I dream of being. This book has two major strengths. First, it lives up to its name! The stories, questions, and tools make leadership within arm's reach for literally *anyone*! Second, Stephen is a very winsome writer. He is an expert on the topic but isn't afraid to show his scars. In some ways, the practices felt like he was sharing the steering wheel. You'll learn and want to do as you read. Let this book mentor you!

—*Preston Ulmer*
Director and Founder of The Doubters' Club

DEDICATION

To Karen,
Leading with you brings me great joy.
I love you!

ACKNOWLEDGMENTS

Thank you, Karen, for your constant love and your faithful encouragement. With this book, as with every book, you have been my greatest support. Leading with you is a true joy. Thank you for believing in me. I love you.

Thank you, Ashley, Dylan, Elijah, and Wyatt. You bring joy to our hearts. May this book inspire you to lead with excellence in everything God calls you to pursue. We're cheering you on.

Thank you, Mom, for your constant prayers and support. Your strength and spiritual fortitude are a gift, and your commitment to the Lord, a life of character, and a passion for prayer inspire us all.

Thank you, 7 City Church, for the honor to serve as your pastor and for the way you lead and serve. My prayer is that this book inspires you to serve with excellence and equips you to lead for the glory of God and the good of others.

Thank you, Martijn van Tilborgh and the team at AVAIL, for believing in this project. Your excellence in publishing is deeply appreciated.

Thank You, Jesus, for your wisdom and grace throughout this project. You are faithful and good in every way. And thank You for the call to steward leadership in a way that truly matters. May this work bring You glory.

CONTENTS

Acknowledgments .... *ix*

Confessions of a Follower .... *xiii*

PART 1. MASTER THE ART OF LEADING YOURSELF 17

CHAPTER 1. How to Grow You 19

CHAPTER 2. How to Be a Spiritually Grounded Leader 35

CHAPTER 3. How to Lead With Character 51

CHAPTER 4. How to Think Like a Leader 71

CHAPTER 5. How to Manage Your Time 93

CHAPTER 6. How to Make Leadership Decisions 113

PART 2. MASTER THE ART OF LEADING OTHERS 133

CHAPTER 7. How to Build Influence 135

CHAPTER 8. How to Lead People 157

CHAPTER 9. How to Be a Servant Leader 179

CHAPTER 10. How to Communicate With People 203

CHAPTER 11. How to Lead Through Conflict 223

CHAPTER 12. How to Coach Others 243

Endnotes *255*

About the Author *265*

Resources *267*

CONFESSIONS OF A FOLLOWER

I'm not a natural leader.

That's probably not a confession you expected to hear right out of the gate. But it's true. Growing up, I was never the popular kid in school. I wasn't the first one picked—or even in the top half—when my classmates chose teams on the playground. I made average grades, was never elected to student council, and nobody labeled me "Most likely to succeed." I was a follower, not a leader.

My first attempt to lead happened when I started a Bible study at my high school. It was a train wreck. A few reluctant students came to the first meeting, but it didn't take long for the participation to dwindle. When I tried to restart the Bible study during my senior year, our sponsor teacher recommended we hold elections to choose the president of the club. She saw my leadership blind spots, but my insecurity got the best of me, and I snubbed her suggestion. The Bible club was *my* idea. Why on earth would we hold an election?

My leadership didn't get much better when I started working at a church. In many ways, it felt like an experiment in blunders and stupidity. In my early years of ministry, I took a group of students to a summer youth camp. There was only one problem—I failed to reserve a trailer to haul the students' luggage. We only had one empty seat in the church van, so I sheepishly announced, "Hey everyone, you may need to hold your luggage in your lap while we drive to camp." The campground was three hours away. When we finally arrived, my attitude made it clear: *I don't want to be here.* The camp director called me out on it, and rightly so.

My lack of leadership genius was evident in other ministry failings as well. Once, I tested a flash pot as a special effect for an upcoming outreach event. The flash pot was a small container that held pyrotechnic powder and was ignited by a tiny wire when you plugged it in. We tested it once, and the "explosion" was awesome. So, we decided to test it again, but this time with *more* powder. To my utter shock, I set a pew on fire—just twelve months after the auditorium had been remodeled. A giant hole, the size of my fist, burned through the seat cushion.

After our "rehearsal," I began driving home, but I was so scared that I returned to the church to make sure nothing else was quietly smoldering under a pew. Then, I called my pastor to break the news. He was gracious in his response, but I can only imagine the dismay that went through his mind.

On another occasion, I reprimanded a group of students for behaving poorly during a meeting. I became so frustrated that I turned around and walked out of the room. Afterward, my wife was quick to tell me, "Thanks for leaving me in the room to clean up your mess." And my pastor made it abundantly clear I could have handled that situation much better. Failure was a close companion in my early days of ministry, and *nobody* hailed me as a natural-born leader.

Turns out, I'm not alone.

Extensive research reveals that only 10 percent of people possess the raw talent to manage.[1] And while there are clear differences between leading and managing, Gallup merges the two by defining a manager as "someone responsible for leading a team toward common objectives."[2]

That's not me.

I'm not a *natural* leader.

Instead, I'm a *learned* leader.[3]

I learned everything I know about leadership by watching other leaders, reading countless books on leadership, attending leadership conferences, acquiring leadership coaching, pursuing a master's in organizational leadership, and—most importantly—*practicing leadership*.

I'm not a *natural* leader; nevertheless, I've become a *very effective* learned leader—which I later discovered has its advantages. I once heard John Maxwell—a great natural leader—say that learned leaders are very good at *teaching and coaching leadership*. Why? Because they had to figure it out for themselves. Through trial and error, coaching and training, and the ups and downs of leadership, they learned how to lead and, therefore, know how to teach leadership in a clear, systematic, and easy-to-understand way.

So, what is leadership?

Good leadership is the ability to positively influence people toward a shared vision while maximizing their gifts for the greater good. Over the years, I've not only learned a host of leadership skills to do just that—such as vision casting, building influence, developing teams, and coaching others—but I've also discovered how to make leadership insanely practical. Whether it's developing an easy-to-understand system or breaking leadership skills into a step-by-step process, I've learned how to put handles on leadership that anyone can use.

If you're a *natural* leader, you're about to discover an insanely practical tool to help you develop the leaders around you. You'll find leadership principles and tactics put into words that come so naturally for you. And, of course, you'll learn some helpful tips to refine your leadership genius.

If you're a *learned* leader, you'll find an insanely practical game plan to become a very effective leader. The content is filled with helpful tips, practical systems, powerful leadership examples, and great application ideas to help you put into practice everything you're learning. You'll elevate your leadership game, and, like natural leaders, you'll hold a roadmap to develop others.

Every chapter is a "how to" chapter packed with insights and tools to equip you for success. If you prefer, you can read the entire book in the order it's written. Or, if you're experiencing an immediate pain point, feel free to jump to the chapter that's most relevant at this moment. Either way, you'll learn some insanely practical skills to maximize your leadership and invest in the people around you. Let's get started.

PART 1
MASTER THE ART OF LEADING YOURSELF

CHAPTER 1

HOW TO GROW YOU

"Growth for leaders is the treasure that funds the future journey. Stop finding the treasure along the way and the journey ends."
—Ken Blanchard and Mark Miller

"I don't want you to hold anything back when you edit my book."

That's what I said to the editor of my first book, *GO! Starting a Personal Growth Revolution*.[4] A mutual friend introduced me to Brannon, an editor with black-belt skills in the English language. He had worked with a successful author of best-selling titles, so I was beyond excited to meet him.

During our first conversation, Brannon gave me clear instructions: "Send me your strongest chapter and your weakest chapter. I'll edit them, and then you can decide if you want to work with me." Before we hung up the phone, I issued my confident challenge to Brannon to hold nothing back as he edited my book.

But his response was just as confident. Without flinching, Brannon said, "Oh, I won't."

And he didn't.

I sent Brannon three chapters and then patiently awaited his glowing editorial commentary. A couple of weeks later, I received Brannon's reply and anxiously opened the file attached to his email.

My heart sank.

Every page—nearly every sentence—was shredded. He used Microsoft Word's "track changes" feature to make his corrections. There were so many comments in the margins that I had to double, triple, and sometimes quadruple-click to open the comment boxes and see the extent of the damage. Brannon bled all over my manuscript, and I was embarrassed.

At first, I thought, *Who does he think he is? Does he know how hard I've worked on this book? Does he have any idea how much blood, sweat, and tears I've shed over this manuscript?*

But editors don't edit to make you happy. They edit to make you better.

After reading his corrections and comments on each chapter, I had to make a decision: will I let my pride hold me back or let Brannon move me forward?

After careful consideration, I said to myself, *Stephen, you're writing a book about personal growth. If you can't handle the pain of a professional editor's wisdom and feedback—pain intended to help you grow—then you shouldn't be writing a book about personal growth.*

So, I reached out to Brannon and thanked him for his feedback. "I want you to edit the remainder of my book," I said. "But first, I want to rewrite each chapter based on the insights you shared with me from the first three chapters."

And that's what I did.

I rewrote *every* chapter based on what Brannon taught me.

My writing improved, and when I finished each chapter, I sent it to Brannon. But the pain that followed was no less severe. It didn't take long for Brannon's editorial genius to leave scraps of my manuscript on the cutting room floor. And not just a few scraps. The floor was covered like a battlefield strewn with dead bodies.

> **Instead of lowering the manuscript to the level of my writing, Brannon pulled the latent potential out of me so my message could fly.**

I found myself divorcing sentences, paragraphs, and even big ideas I was once married to. Brannon didn't just wordsmith each chapter. He murdered my manuscript. But when the agony ended, he helped me resurrect a message in a voice I didn't know I had. He pulled the potential out of me that I couldn't see in myself.

Every cut and every comment made me better. Every slice and slash, every revision and renovation, brought what seemed doomed back to life. Instead of lowering the manuscript to the level of my writing, Brannon pulled the latent potential out of me so my message could fly.

When I finished the book, I wrote in the acknowledgments, "Brannon: Thank you for your masterful work with words. You have been more than an editor to me.... You've been a mentor."

Brannon didn't just correct typos or tell me how to structure sentences better. He helped me find my voice. And every book since then has benefited from the wisdom I gleaned in that very first project.

I hate to think what would have happened if I ignored Brannon's advice. I'm confident of this—I would have never raised the lid on my growth as a writer.

HOW TO GROW YOU

As a leader, you are responsible for *owning* your growth. You can't delegate it or negotiate it. You can't relegate it or vacate it. Growth is a permanent task in every job description at every level of the organization. If growth is ever checked off your to-do list, you'll be done with far more than you bargained for.

Ken Blanchard and Mark Miller once said, "Growth for leaders is the treasure that funds the future journey. Stop finding the treasure along the way and the journey ends."[5] Sadly, some leaders have stopped mining for the treasure. Others are looking for it haphazardly and half-heartedly. Still, others have bankrupted their future because they made personal growth optional.

As a leader, you have a dream burning in your gut. But between you and your dream is a gap—a growth gap. The only way to close that gap is to fund the journey toward your dream with the treasure of your growth. This happens when you get insanely practical about three keys: a growth mindset, a growth plan, and a growth team.

1) Adopt a Growth Mindset

When Karen and I got married, she had a two-year college degree and worked as an administrative assistant at a local hospital.

In the years that followed, she served in a variety of roles before finally applying to become a ticket agent for a major airline. The onboarding process for that job required six weeks of intensive training, but to Karen's surprise, she aced the training. However, that onboarding experience turned out to be far more than a job opportunity. It awakened a growth mindset in Karen and gave her the confidence to reenroll in college to complete a bachelor's degree.

On the first day of class, she was so nervous that she almost dropped out. She hadn't sat in a college classroom for more than a decade, and she wasn't sure she could cut it. But after that first class, she never looked back. Over the next three years, Karen worked hard to earn a history degree to become a teacher in the public school system.

On the day she graduated, her growth mindset didn't drift off to sleep. Quite the opposite. As she watched master's students cross the stage to receive their diplomas, she said to herself, *One day, that will be me.* And one day, it was. She taught for several years and then began the arduous journey of pursuing a master's in counseling. She worked all day and went to classes at night at TCU—all while being a mom and a pastor's wife. After four years, she graduated with her master's and then became a school counselor.

When you graduate school, a robust growth mindset won't let you graduate learning. In the years that followed her graduation, Karen's lifelong learning posture fueled a dream to become a licensed professional counselor. She completed some additional classes and then started the long process of certification. After completing three thousand hours of counseling, her dream finally came true.

Today, Karen has her own counseling practice, and she loves it. She reached her goal because she never checked a growth mindset off her list. It's the driver in the seat of your potential. Since becoming an LPC, Karen has continued to acquire new counseling certifications, and every morning, I can hear her listening to podcasts, books, and interviews to sharpen her skills. That's the power of a growth mindset. As author Michael Hyatt observed, "Our beliefs about what's possible have a direct impact on the reality we experience."[6]

For our dreams to move from hopeful aspirations to vivid reality, we must adopt a growth mindset. Jesus provides us with a powerful example: "Jesus grew in wisdom and in stature and in favor with God and all the people" (Luke 2:52). Notice that Jesus's growth was intentional and continual. He didn't think about growing—He grew. And He wasn't haphazard about growing—He grew mentally, physically, spiritually, and socially.

> **For a growth mindset to take root in your life, you must give an eviction notice to the limiting beliefs that are holding you back.**

That's the kind of growth mindset we need—one that's intentional and continual. Without it, we'll view growth as nothing more than a one-time event. Events, such as conferences and seminars, are great at *inspiring* change, but the change doesn't actually happen at the event. A process of growth must follow the event to produce sustainable, long-term habits of transformation. Simply put, events inspire change, processes create change, and habits sustain change.

This process is painful. As author and consultant Dr. Sam Chand observes, "You will grow only to the threshold of your pain."[7] Growth is only found on the other side of pain if you have the right mindset. Your mindset will determine whether the pain becomes a cap or a catalyst for your growth.

For a growth mindset to take root in your life, you must give an eviction notice to the limiting beliefs that are holding you back. When you believe your life can change, you'll start growing toward that change. Otherwise, who you are today will be all you'll ever know. As author Erwin McManus observed, "Most limitations are illusions created by our inner fears, doubts, and insecurities. It requires a mind shift to see that the ceiling is not actually there."[8] You must believe more is possible. You must recognize that the growth gap doesn't have to be a permanent gap. It all starts with your mindset.

2) Create a Growth Plan

As a teenager, throughout college, and at the start of my career, I didn't enjoy reading, which is kind of ironic for a person who writes books. Not until I was a couple of years into my leadership journey did I finally admit I was only hurting myself by neglecting a habit of reading. I've shared my journey in previous books, so I'll keep it short.

One day, I picked up the first edition of John Maxwell's book *Developing the Leader Within You*.[9] I devoured the book, and after reading it, I said, "I think this is the best leadership book I've ever read."

That's when it dawned on me.

"I think this is the *only* leadership book I've ever read."

But that book became a launching pad for my personal growth. It awakened a growth mindset in me, and I began consuming more and more leadership content.

As my growth mindset took root, I attended a lunch gathering with three hundred leaders to hear John Maxwell teach from his book *The 21 Irrefutable Laws of Leadership*[10] (again, this was the original edition). That day, he taught "The Law of Process," which says, "Leadership develops daily, not in a day." Then, at the conclusion of the lunch, he challenged his audience to develop a plan for personal growth.

In response to Maxwell's challenge, I bought his kit based on the twenty-one laws, which included a workbook and several cassette tapes. Yes, this was back in the '90s. For my younger readers, I'm sure you can find these historical artifacts in a museum.

Each day I came into the office an hour early, listened to a tape, and took notes in the workbook. That kit became my very first growth plan and helped me close some of my leadership growth gaps.

Since buying that kit many years ago, I've developed a growth planning model that I call a *Growth TRAC*. A Growth TRAC is a specific, measurable, and accountable plan for personal and professional growth.[11] It's a customizable growth planning process that helps you fill your treasure chest so you can fund your dreams with your growth. The TRAC growth planning model helps you answer four growth questions.

TARGET: WHAT ARE MY GROWTH GOALS?

A Growth TRAC first identifies the *Target* you hope to reach. The target pinpoints a specific growth area—spiritual, relational, emotional, mental, financial, vocational, or organizational. This process doesn't require any mental gymnastics because most people have an intuitive sense of where they want to grow and how they want to improve.

Once you identify your growth area, turn it into a target by stating it as a clear goal. For example, your target might be, "Improve my emotional intelligence by 10 percent by September 15" or "Develop my strategic planning skills so I can facilitate a strategic planning retreat with my team by May 20." Each target is clear, specific, measurable, and time-bound.

ROADMAP: HOW DO I PLAN TO GROW?

My wife will tell you I'm directionally challenged. I've been known to turn the wrong way down one-way streets. I'll take wrong exits, turn left when I should turn right, and take shortcuts that turn out to be dead ends. If that's not bad enough, I recently got lost in a parking garage.

To avoid making the same mistake with your personal growth, you need a *Roadmap* to get you to your *target*. Your roadmap will include a series of growth steps, such as training, resources, coaching, and experiences. For example, your roadmap to develop your strategic planning skills might include attending a strategic planning seminar (training), reading a book about strategic planning (resource), meeting with a strategic planning consultant (coaching), and organizing a strategic planning retreat (experience). Each step is part of your roadmap to help you reach your ultimate target.

ACCOUNTABILITY: WHO WILL HOLD ME ACCOUNTABLE FOR MY GROWTH?

Accountability is uncomfortable, which is why it's easy to overlook. You're responsible for your own growth, but accountability helps you leverage the support of friends and mentors. The keys to successful accountability are *focus* and *frequency*.

Focus provides your accountability partner with specific questions focused on your growth. For example, have a friend ask you, "What strategic planning skills have you learned in the last two weeks?" or "How much of your strategic planning book have you read, and what are your three biggest takeaways so far?"

Frequency is how often you meet with your accountability partner—perhaps weekly, monthly, or quarterly. Be consistent. As author Jim Collins observed, "The signature of mediocrity is chronic inconsistency."[12] To keep your Growth TRAC out of the gutter of mediocrity, meet with an accountability partner regularly to help take the growth steps in your roadmap.

CHECK-UP: WHEN AND HOW WILL I EVALUATE MY GROWTH PROGRESS?

The final part of the Growth TRAC is *Check-Ups*. Check-ups help you evaluate and monitor progress, and then make necessary adjustments. To maximize check-ups, you'll want to take four steps. First, attach deadlines to each step in your roadmap. This will help you complete each step on time. Second, conduct your check-ups in a systematic way (monthly, quarterly, or semi-annually), depending on what makes the most sense for your goal.

Third, make mid-course corrections. It's okay to change your Growth TRAC as you discover what's working and what's not.

Fourth, enlist the help of your accountability partner. Include them in the check-up or provide an update to them with your overall progress and any mid-course corrections.

A Growth TRAC will help you create an intentional plan for personal and professional growth. You can also use this process with your team. (For a sample Growth TRAC, see Leadership Tool #1 at the end of this chapter.)

3) Assemble a Growth Team

My friend Scott Wilson introduced me to the idea of a growth team. I've always valued mentors and coaches, but Scott expanded my thinking to form a more robust team that helps me grow in the most important areas of my life. Consider developing a growth team that looks something like this:

At the center of your growth team, write, "God and me." A relationship with God profoundly shapes who we become and how we grow. God shouldn't be an addition to our lives. Instead, He should sit at the core of our lives. Then, surrounding your relationship with God, assemble a growth team to help you become healthy in a variety of areas.

For example, your spouse or a close family member might help you grow in the most important relationships in your life. Prayer partners can help you grow spiritually. A counselor can help you grow emotionally while a host of coaches, mentors, and consultants can elevate your growth at work. Financial advisors provide wisdom on stewarding money and saving for the future. Wise friends help us grow wise, and physical growth is made possible with the help of doctors and workout partners. Each of these people can be part of your growth team.

Where do you start? Begin by identifying the primary roles and responsibilities in your life. Then, identify individuals to help you grow in those specific areas. Invite them to join your growth team, and then determine when and how often you'd like to meet. Keep in mind that some of your team members may require a financial investment, such as counselors, coaches, and consultants.

To create your own growth team, begin by identifying the primary roles and responsibilities in your life. Then, identify individuals to help you grow in those specific areas. Invite them to join your growth team, and then determine when and how often you'd like to meet.

Finally, determine what you need from your growth team. When you meet with them, come prepared with questions, take notes, and then apply what you're learning. Be sure to honor their time and effort.

The members of your growth team will look different based on the roles and responsibilities in your life. Furthermore, some growth team members will change as the needs and seasons of your life change. To help you develop your own growth team, see Leadership Tool #1: Growth TRAC and Growth Team.

These are the keys to insanely practical growth. You must adopt a growth mindset, create a growth plan, and then assemble a growth team. All three will change and mature over time, but they are the core ingredients to develop your potential and maximize your personal and professional growth.

INSANELY PRACTICAL REFLECTION AND DISCUSSION

1. Why is personal growth essential in the life of a leader, and what excuses do we often give for failing to prioritize our growth?
2. What does it look like to have an intentional and continual growth mindset?
3. In what area of your life do you want to create a growth plan, and what steps could you include in your roadmap to grow?
4. If you were to assemble a growth team, who are two people who could help you grow the most?

LEADERSHIP TOOL #1
Growth TRAC and Growth Team

Review the sample Growth TRAC below. Then, create your own Growth TRAC in the template. Choose your Target (goal), create a Roadmap (training, resources, coaching, and experiences), identify someone to hold you Accountable, and establish a Check-Up process.

	GROWTH QUESTION	GROWTH TRAC
T	**TARGET** What is my growth goal?	Create and cast a compelling vision for my department by May 15.
R	**ROADMAP** What is my growth plan?	• Read The Vision Driven Leader by Michael Hyatt. • Create the first draft of a vision. • Share the vision with three leaders and make adjustments on two rounds of input. • Create a vision-casting script and secure feedback from my leadership coach. • Cast vision to my department.
A	**ACCOUNTABILITY** Who will hold me accountable for my growth?	• Accountability Partner: Alan Colson • Accountability Question: What progress have you made on each step to clarify and cast vision to your department?
C	**CHECK-UP** When and how will I evaluate my growth progress?	Evaluate progress as follows: • Read book by January 20 • Create vision draft by February 5 • Secure leadership team input by March 5 • Vision script and coaching by April 15 • Cast vision May 15

	GROWTH QUESTION	GROWTH TRAC
T	**TARGET** What is my growth goal?	
R	**ROADMAP** What is my growth plan?	
A	**ACCOUNTABILITY** Who will hold me accountable for my growth?	
C	**CHECK-UP** When and how will I evaluate my growth progress?	

Use the chart below to assemble your Growth Team. Identify your current roles, a growth team member, how often you'll meet, and the area where you need their help to grow.

GROWTH TEAM			
MY ROLES	GROWTH TEAM MEMBER	FREQUENCY OF MEETING	CURRENT GROWTH NEED

Download the Growth TRAC and Growth Team templates at insanelypracticalleadership.com.

CHAPTER 2

HOW TO BE A SPIRITUALLY GROUNDED LEADER

"When a leader has a lifelong developmental perspective, that leader expects God to shape him over a lifetime. The leader views the things that happen to him as God's sovereign way of developing him."
—Dr. J. Robert Clinton

The year was 1984. Apple unveiled its Macintosh personal computer during a Super Bowl ad, Tina Turner's song, "What's Love Got to Do with It," topped the charts, and the Supreme Court ruled (5-4) that the private use of a home VCR to tape TV programs for later viewing did not violate federal copyright laws.[13] How times have changed.

But for me, 1984 was the year my curiosity about Jesus was fully awakened. I was in ninth grade, and one night after a youth service, I went home, climbed into bed, and then whispered a prayer as I stared at the ceiling: "Jesus, please forgive me of my sin and be the Lord of my life."

There was nothing emotional about that moment. I didn't cry, revel in God's grace, or run victory laps around my bedroom. Nevertheless, that moment marked me. In the days that followed, my appetite to know God grew stronger. Then, at the start of my tenth-grade year, I joined a discipleship class that bolstered my spiritual growth.

Each week, a handful of students met around a couple of eight-foot tables. There weren't any cool games or fun competitions, and the classroom with cinder block walls screamed "boring." In our very first meeting, our youth pastor gave each of us a three-ring binder with lined notebook paper inside it. He said, "This is your quiet time notebook." *Quiet time* was code for "Spend time with God," and our binder was the tool to help us pray and study the Bible.

Looking at a group of wide-eyed students, he continued: "Each day, take a few minutes to read a passage of scripture until you get to a verse that really speaks to you. Then, write down the passage, the key verse, and look up other scripture references that reinforce it."

Simple enough, I thought. *I can do this.*

"Then, write down the main truths you learned from the passage," he said, "along with how you'll apply them to your life." That was our roadmap to study the Bible. With those simple instructions, we started with the gospel of John.

I still have that old, vinyl three-ring binder. My very first entry was on Thursday, September 6, 1984. And in the months that followed, I studied four books of the Bible: John, Galatians, Matthew, and Ephesians.

That class changed my life.

That practice ignited within me a love for God's Word.
That habit spiritually grounded me.
But my spiritual training didn't end there.

EARLY MORNINGS

A couple of years later, our pastor began opening the church's sanctuary on weekday mornings at 6:00 a.m. for prayer. This wasn't a corporate prayer gathering with dozens of congregants but a place for people to privately pray at the start of each day. Some people knelt in prayer while others sat quietly in a pew. Some lay on the floor calling out to God while others would pace and pray throughout the dimly lit auditorium.

> **Looking back, I now realize prayer is more caught than taught, and I was beginning to catch their habit of prayer.**

A couple of times each week, a friend stopped by my house to pick me up for early morning prayer. As I sat in the quietness of the sanctuary, I could hear various pastors praying. I heard their cries, their burdens, their hunger to know God. I heard them pour out their hearts as they asked God to pour out His Spirit. Those prayers were expressed with a beautiful blend of love for God and compassion for people.

In the weeks that followed, I found myself mimicking these prayers. I wasn't trying to copy them, but I had never learned how to pray. Their practice of prayer became a model for me to follow. Looking back, I now realize prayer is more *caught* than *taught*, and I was beginning to catch their habit of prayer.

Those two encounters changed the trajectory of my life. Learning how to study the Bible as a pimple-nosed teenager and developing my own habit of prayer spiritually grounded me. While I didn't know it at the time, those habits also became the foundation of my leadership.

Today, I start most mornings studying my Bible and spending time in prayer. I walk into the kitchen, make a cup of coffee, and then sit down at the kitchen table with my Bible and journal. After reading my Bible, I open my journal, jot down three things I'm grateful for, and then write my reflections on the passage of scripture I just read. It's a peaceful and powerful way to start my morning. And one day, I'll give those journals to my grandsons.

Next, I spend some time in prayer. Sometimes, I sit, sometimes, I kneel, and sometimes, I pace and pray, walking circles around our living room. Sometimes, I'll read a "daily declaration" to renew my mind in God's Word. And sometimes, I'll simply worship.

Regular prayer and consistent Bible study—not to prepare a sermon but to simply know Jesus more deeply—are the sustaining sources of a lifetime of leadership. Nothing else can replace them.

HOW TO BE A SPIRITUALLY GROUNDED LEADER

Leadership is immensely challenging. Just this week, I talked to a pastor with a bold vision to plant a new church, a minister lamenting the heart-breaking pain of a board member gone rogue, a missionary navigating transition as a veteran leader passes the baton, and a church planter experiencing extreme spiritual warfare in an urban context. Every situation comes with its share of stress and struggle.

As the external pressures of leadership increase, we need a more powerful presence within us. My strength isn't enough. Neither is yours. That's why the apostle Paul said, "I pray that from his glorious, unlimited resources he will empower you with inner strength through his Spirit" (Ephesians 3:16). Without the unlimited resources of the Holy Spirit, we'll navigate the landmines of leadership in the limitations of our own strength. Eventually, we'll burn out, blow up, or wither in exasperation. To tap those unlimited resources and become a spiritually grounded leader, we need four spiritual keys.

1) Spiritual Priority

Author Greg McKeown made an interesting observation about the word *priority*. McKeown notes that when the word priority came into the English language in the 1400s, it was originally a singular word that meant "the prior or very first thing." It remained a singular word for the next five hundred years, until the 1900s when we made the term plural: *priorities*. McKeown poses a powerful question: can there be *multiple very first things*?[14]

Unfortunately, many people are convinced the answer to McKeown's question is a decisive "Yes"—even in their spiritual lives. But you can't swear your allegiance to multiple first gods. There is only one God, and Jesus makes it painstakingly clear what priority He must have in our lives: "But *seek first* his kingdom and his righteousness, and all these things will be given to you as well" (Matthew 6:33, NIV, emphasis added).

> **Jesus must not only be first; He must also be the center.**

Prior to this verse, Jesus addresses the wants and worries our hearts long for. But rather than being dominated by our *want for things* and the *worries of life*, Jesus calls us to seek first His kingdom and righteousness. To seek His kingdom means to seek His kingship in and over our lives. And to seek His righteousness is to seek a life conformed to the righteousness of Christ. When we do this, He promises to take care of our wants and worries (Matthew 6:33).

This is the starting place to become a spiritually grounded leader. Seeking God must be our *very first thing*. But let me take it one step further: Jesus must not only be first; He must also be the *center*.

We love lists, and if you follow a time-management system, you probably have a robust list of tasks to do, people to see, and projects to finish. One by one, we complete our tasks and then proudly put a check by each one.

Take the kids to school. *Check.*
Complete the project at work. *Check.*
Lead the staff meeting. *Check.*
Pick up the laundry. *Check.*
Wrap the birthday present. *Check.*
Mow the lawn. *Check.*
Make dinner. *Check.*

Each check gives us permission to move on to something else that requires our attention. But let me be clear: putting Jesus first doesn't reduce Him to the first task on our to-do list. Tasks get checked off the list. Jesus doesn't. Instead, He influences everything on the list.

Simply put, Jesus must be the *center* of our lives.

When Jesus is the center, He influences every other part of our lives. He influences our work, family, relationships, hobbies, time, talent, and treasure. We seek Him *first*, and He sits at the *center* of our lives, influencing everything else.

What about you? Do you seek Jesus first? Does He sit at the center of your life with permission to freely influence the rest of your life? Becoming spiritually grounded begins when our lives are grounded in Jesus. It's making Him your Priority—your very first thing.

2) Spiritual Practices

Years ago, news anchor Dan Rather interviewed Mother Teresa. In the interview, he asked, "When you pray, what do you say to God?" Mother Teresa's response was unexpected: "I don't say anything. I listen."

Curious to know more, Dan Rather asked, "Well, okay... when God speaks to you, then, what does He say?"

Mother Teresa replied, "He doesn't say anything. He listens."

The news anchor was puzzled. Then, she added, "And if you don't understand that, I can't explain it to you."[15]

Mother Teresa's words sound perplexing, but in the most beautiful way, she's describing friendship with God. Sometimes, friends just quietly sit with each other. Their presence is enough.

Spiritual practices bring us into the presence of Jesus. Author Richard Foster described it powerfully:

We do indeed engage in practices—disciplines, if you will—but remember, these practices earn us nothing in the economy of God. Nothing. Their only purpose is to place us before God. That is all. . . . God then steps into our actions and, over time and experience, produces in us the formation of heart and mind and soul for which we long.[16]

Notice that spiritual practices don't change us—God does. The practices are merely the way we place ourselves before God so He can do His work of transformation inside our hearts.

Spiritual practices take various shapes and sizes. Prayer, Bible study, worship, fasting, serving, generosity, and community are just a few of those practices that bring us before God to be transformed by His presence. When those practices are employed deliberately and consistently, the transformation is deep and wide. Not only are we changed, but those around us are changed as well.

My grandmother—Violet Morley—understood the power of spiritual practices, particularly the practice of prayer. She lived in Lakenheath, England, but her prayer life wasn't contained to the limits of this tiny village. One day, I felt prompted to call and ask her about the lessons she had learned from a lifetime of prayer. That day, she said something I'll never forget: "We have to do many different things, but *prayer* is the main thing."

There it is again—the very first thing.

Prayer was her priority.

Grandma lived to be ninety-two years old, and although she was small in stature, her prayer life was enormous in impact. In fact, at her funeral, stories were told and letters were read by the people Grandma quite literally "prayed into the Kingdom." Her impact was so deep that on three separate occasions, people stood in applause. I've been to a lot of funerals, but I've never seen the person in the casket receive a standing ovation. Grandma's life was like a ripple, and prayer was the engine that produced each ripple.

That's the beauty of a life devoted to prayer, God's Word, and the practices that foster spiritual maturity.

What about you? What are you doing to cultivate spiritual practices that draw you close to Jesus, fuel your spirit, settle your mind, and empower your leadership? Maybe it's time to deliberately and consistently increase your engagement in spiritual practices.

3) Spiritual Pace

I've always valued time with God, but over the past few years, the Lord has been teaching me the power and importance of *unrushed* time with God. This might sound like a trivial discrepancy, but in a culture consumed with getting more done in less time, I believe it's the difference-maker—especially for leaders with heavy demands.

Jesus was one such leader.

After performing a miracle where He fed five thousand people, Jesus insisted His disciples get into a boat and cross the lake. Then, after sending the crowds home, "He went up into the hills by himself to pray. Night fell while he was there alone" (Matthew 14:23). But the disciples didn't immediately follow Jesus's instructions. Instead, "That evening Jesus' disciples went down to the shore *to wait for him*. But as darkness fell and *Jesus still hadn't come back*, they got into the boat and headed across the lake toward Capernaum" (John 6:16-17, emphasis added).

> **If we're not careful, we'll begin measuring intimacy with God by our efficiency with God.**

Those passages sound simple enough, but when I read them, I'm convicted with this thought: *Has anyone ever had to wait on me to finish praying?* Jesus modeled *the unrushed way* by not rushing His time with the Father. Despite the demands Jesus faced, His leadership pace didn't exceed His spiritual pace.

I know; *unrushed* time with God sounds irrational and impossible, especially when speed is the name of the game for so many leaders. But if we're not careful, we'll begin measuring intimacy with God by our efficiency with God. Efficiency sounds like a good leadership tactic, but intimacy is the fuel to help you finish well.

Authors Ryan Skoog, Peter Greer, and Cameron Doolittle rightly note the importance of pace to fight the intoxicating nature of leadership influence: "One of the easiest ways to fight the temptation to value influence above God is to lead at the *pace of prayer*. We may be worshiping the idol of influence rather than Jesus if we and those we lead are too busy serving Jesus to have a dynamic prayer life."[17]

When we combine spiritual practices with a healthy spiritual pace, the transformation is deep. You can't microwave maturity. It requires a spiritual pace that makes room for our soul to breathe and the Spirit to work.

4) Spiritual Perspective

In the year 2000, after spending eleven years in local church youth ministry, a friend and I teamed up to launch an organization to train young leaders. Each year, we conducted dozens of events around the United States to train thousands of leaders. We created leadership curriculum, conducted an innovative leadership experience in Europe, and even trained students in places like Germany and Japan.

Starting this ministry required a big step of faith. In addition to building something from the ground up, most of our staff had to raise their own financial support—much like a missionary. For the first eighteen months, Karen and I lived with my in-laws just to make ends meet, and there were multiple times when we had to pick and choose which bill to pay first. We loved our mission, but in the end, the organization didn't survive.

When you work extremely hard to bring a dream to life, and then you watch it die a slow death, your mind is ravaged with questions—many of which go unanswered. To make matters worse, other people ask you questions too. "Why didn't the ministry make it?" "How come it no longer exists?" "What was the point of all that?"

But as I look back on the four years that I served the organization, I now see through a different set of lenses. In many ways—and my coworkers would agree—God did His greatest work *in* us during that time. How so? For me personally, it was during that season:

- I learned to trust God in a deeper measure.
- I discovered my purpose in life and was able to articulate it in a life-mission statement.
- I learned the power of personal growth planning.
- I came to understand how God shapes and forms leaders.
- My knowledge of leadership skyrocketed.
- My philosophy of leadership was significantly shaped by Scripture.

I'm the leader I am today in large part because of that difficult season. In fact, I've written two books since then that would not exist today had I not gone through that journey. Furthermore, the vision of the church I pastor today was highly influenced by what I learned during those four pivotal years.

On the outside, most people would call it a failure. If I wanted to, I could certainly choose to interpret it that way too. Instead, I choose to see it with a lifelong developmental perspective. Leadership expert Dr. J. Robert Clinton describes it like this:

> *When a leader has a lifelong developmental perspective, that leader expects God to shape him over a lifetime. The leader views the things that happen to him as God's sovereign way of developing him. That leader recognizes that all of life, while being vital and true for the moment, is also used to prepare him for all of the rest of life.*[18]

Please stop and reread Dr. Clinton's words.

Now, do it again.

Spiritually grounded leaders "expect" God's shaping activity throughout their lives. Leaders committed to spiritual maturity view hardships, tests, and trials as "God's sovereign way of developing" them. Leaders with spiritual perspective realize that "all of life" will "prepare [them] for all of the rest of life." This is why spiritual perspective is so crucial to your leadership. Without it, not only will you see hardship incorrectly, but you'll squander the work of God inside you.

To lead for a lifetime, you need a lifetime developmental perspective. You need to see pain, tests, and trials as the tools God uses to form you, grow you, and stretch you as a leader. I'm not suggesting God is the originator of all these hardships, but God doesn't waste them either. The question is, will you?

Joseph is a perfect case study of spiritual perspective. He was sold by his brothers into slavery, falsely accused of attempted rape, and thrown in prison for years. After thirteen years of rejection, accusation, and imprisonment, Joseph was miraculously promoted to second-in-command of Egypt.

When a devastating famine struck the land, Joseph's brothers came searching for food. When they knelt before Joseph, pleading for food and the opportunity to return safely home, Joseph didn't take revenge on his brothers. Instead, his spiritual perspective won the day: "You intended to harm me, but God intended it all for good. He brought me to this position so I could save the lives of many people" (Genesis 50:20).

This is the kind of perspective you need when the clouds of pain and suffering come rolling in. This is the outlook you must take when you're betrayed, rejected, and falsely accused. But it can only happen if you adopt a spiritual perspective—one that believes "God intended it all for good."

Without a healthy spiritual perspective, you risk becoming angry, bitter, and resentful at the very pain God wants to redeem to shape you into a Christ-centered leader. Without spiritual perspective, your heart will grow cold, and you'll become resistant to the voice of His Spirit.

Is it hard? Certainly! But as the apostle Paul once said, "Easy street is a dead-end street" (Philippians 3:17-19, MSG). Don't undermine God's work inside you just because your leadership circumstances are unenjoyable, undesirable, and unbearable. A more spiritually grounded version of you—deeply in love with Jesus—awaits on the other side of the pain if you'll view it with the right perspective.

Dr. J. Robert Clinton further emphasized the importance of perspective when he said, "The difference between leaders and followers is perspective. The difference between leaders and effective leaders is better perspective."[19] A *spiritual* perspective gives you the *better* perspective. It helps you frame hardship correctly and respond to life wisely.

Priority makes your spiritual growth important. Practices make your spiritual growth evident. Pace makes your spiritual growth vibrant. Perspective makes your spiritual growth resilient. This is the pathway to becoming a spiritually grounded leader. Together, these ingredients will deepen your trust in God and form you into a spiritually mature leader. To put these keys into practice, begin with Leadership Tool #2: The Spiritual Maturity Map.

INSANELY PRACTICAL REFLECTION AND DISCUSSION

1. What or whom has God used to inspire or accelerate your spiritual journey?
2. Which spiritual practice has most profoundly shaped your spiritual growth, and which practice would you like to grow in?
3. What would it look like for you to cultivate "unrushed time with God"?
4. How does a spiritual perspective help you process hardship, navigate pain, and keep your heart tender before God?

LEADERSHIP TOOL #2
The Spiritual Maturity Map

Use the Spiritual Maturity Map below to assess the four keys to becoming a spiritually grounded leader and to develop a plan to foster deeper spiritual maturity.

SPIRITUAL MATURITY MAP		
SPIRITUAL PRIORITY: On a scale from 1 to 10, how much of a priority is your spiritual growth right now?		
1 2 3 4 5 6 7 8 9 10		
SPIRITUAL PRACTICES: Pick two spiritual practices you'd like to give concentrated focus to over the next thirty days. Articulate below when and how you will do this.		
Prayer	Community	Evangelism
Bible Study	Serving	Fasting
Worship	Generosity	Solitude
How will you cultivate these spiritual practices?		
SPIRITUAL PACE: What are some practical steps you can take to slow your pace to create unrushed time with God?		
SPIRITUAL PERSPECTIVE: Which of the statements below best describes how you typically view tests, trials, and hardships in your life?		
	I view tests, trials, and hardships as I'm doing something wrong.	
	I view tests, trials, and hardships as an attack from the devil.	
	I view tests, trials, and hardships as God's disappointment in me.	
	I view tests, trials, and hardships as just a part of normal life.	
	I view tests, trials, and hardships as part of God's life-shaping process.	
What changes do you need to make in your perspective on tests, trials, and hardships, and how can you develop greater cooperation with God's life-shaping process?		

Download the Spiritual Maturity Map at
insanelypracticalleadership.com.

CHAPTER 3

HOW TO LEAD WITH CHARACTER

"We plant sod where God wants us to plant seed. He's more interested in growing our character than having us look finished."
—Bob Goff

On May 8, 1981, late into the evening, Mae Rose Williams heard a big "swoosh" outside of her home in Winter Park, Florida. Mae's dog started barking as a sinkhole opened near the intersection of South Denning Drive and West Fairbanks Avenue. Over the next forty-eight hours, a giant crater formed more than three hundred feet wide and eighty feet deep.

When the destruction ended, the sinkhole had caused more than $4 million in damage as it gobbled up Williams's three-bedroom wood frame home, part of a city swimming pool, and five Porsches from a nearby German auto shop.[20] Camera crews arrived from around the nation, and it even became a short-lived tourist attraction featuring commemorative "Sinkhole '81" T-shirts.[21]

Once the ground finally stabilized, the city used cranes to remove the cars and Williams's home from the giant sinkhole before filling it in with dirt and concrete.[22] Today, it's the site of Lake Rose, named in honor of Mae Rose Williams, who passed away in 2005.

> **Sinkholes aren't confined to land. They also find their way into our character as leaders.**

How do sinkholes form?

In the case of the Winter Park sinkhole, research by a city engineer revealed that rainfall after a dry period triggered the sinkhole.[23] The United States Geological Survey further notes that sinkholes form when rock below the surface of the land dissolves due to groundwater circulating around it. When this happens, spaces and caverns form underground until the surface of the land collapses.[24] Sinkholes leave a wake of destruction and permanently change the landscape.

Unfortunately, sinkholes aren't confined to land. They also find their way into our character as leaders.

When our souls become dry, the rains of pressure and problems cause subtle character cracks to become giant sinkholes. When the waters of compromise circulate in our hearts, over time, our character dissolves. Eventually, a sinkhole opens and takes us down.

Every time I see a leader fall, my heart grieves. I'm saddened for them, their family, and the organization they've led for so many years. I'm especially broken for the victims who have suffered because of their poor choices or abusive behavior. And when you're close to a leader who has fallen, the stages of grief come flooding into your heart.

The grief begins with a period of denial as you struggle to accept what has happened. But as reality sets in, anger takes over. You get mad at the person who broke your trust. You blame people who enabled their behavior. You might even be angry with God. Before long, you start bargaining with yourself: *If only I had seen the signs* or *God, if You'll turn this around, I promise I'll be kinder and less critical.* But as the grief is prolonged, depression sets in, and feelings of hopelessness and sadness settle in our souls. Our energy dips, we can't sleep, and we lose interest in our normal activities. But eventually, after a prolonged period, we accept the loss and find the strength to move forward with our lives.

A friend once shared with me a helpful perspective from his counselor about the stages of grief. He said, "The stages are more like steps." In other words, you don't move through the stages of grief in a linear process. You might take three steps forward and then find yourself stepping back into anger or denial. Back and forth you go until acceptance finally takes root.

Our lack of character doesn't just impact us. It leaves a wake of collateral damage as lives are destroyed, families grieve, teams dismantle, and entire organizations collapse. But the sinkhole always starts inside us, and it begins when our character comes under agonizing pressure.

CHARACTER UNDER PRESSURE

Character is the foundation of leadership. In the same way that we don't trust the ground beneath our feet when a giant sinkhole opens, we don't trust leaders when a cavern is exposed in their character.

Yes, we've heard the platitudes a million times before:

"Lead by example."

"Practice what you preach."

"Don't be a hypocrite."

And yet, leaders are crashing at an alarming rate.

It's not hard to understand why. Expectations to perform are at an all-time high. If your organization's growth isn't up and to the right month after month, you're made to feel something must be wrong—with *you*. If somebody is disgruntled with you or your organization, they don't hesitate to blast you on social media, post a scathing review, or even cancel you. Mounting pressure combined with unrealistic expectations chips away at the foundation of character.

Each chip creates more cracks. Each criticism creates more cynicism. Before long, our character can no longer support the weight of our leadership.

When this happens, leaders often lie to themselves.

"I deserve a break."

"A little fun never hurt anyone."

"They don't understand what it's like."

The problem is that lies lead to lapses in judgment. The more lies we tell ourselves, the more those lies turn into underground currents that erode the rock of our character. When the lie is exposed, everything we lead collapses as the people around us watch in disbelief. As author Lance Witt observed, "When leaders neglect their interior life, they run the risk of prostituting the sacred gift of leadership. And they run the risk of being destructive instead of productive."[25]

HOW TO LEAD WITH CHARACTER

Every leader has a source that powers their influence. Your source of influence might be your position or title, your expertise in a specific topic or field, or your depth of relationship with others. There's nothing inherently wrong with any of these sources of influence. A title will get you in the door and buy you a little bit of time to prove what kind of leader you really are. Expertise adds immense value to people as they learn from your pool of knowledge. And the people you influence the most are usually those with whom you have the closest relationship.

But the most powerful source of influence is our *character*. Who we are—our character, integrity, and spirituality—is the most enduring source for influencing others.

So, how do you *lead with character*? Truth be told, there are multiple layers to it—five to be exact. The journey begins deep inside of us but has the potential to multiply around us. When we understand each layer, we can use our character as the primary source of influence for the good of others and the glory of God. Let's take a closer look at each of the five layers of leading with character.

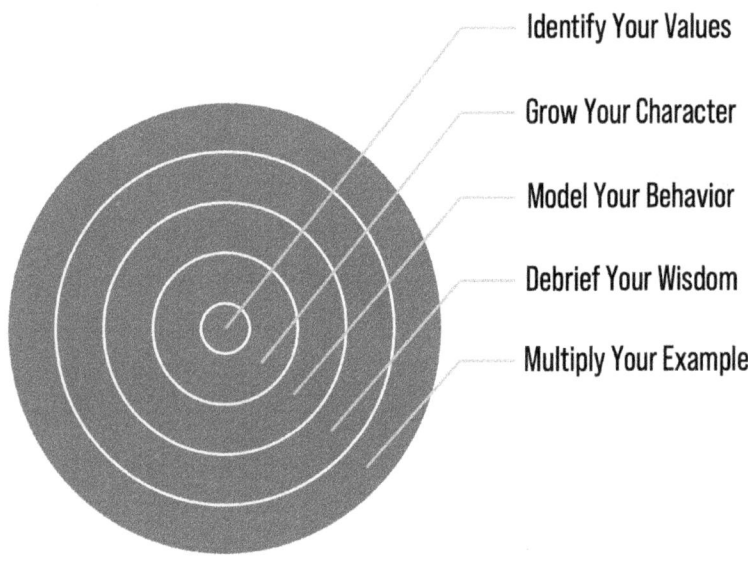

Layer #1: Identify Your Values

Leading with character begins by knowing your values. Values are your character compass that points you in the right direction. Values are formed at the intersection of our beliefs, principles, and priorities.

Beliefs are the core set of creeds and convictions that anchor our lives. For followers of Jesus, beliefs are grounded in Scripture and provide a firm foundation for character development.

Principles are wisdom and guardrails that guide us down the right path. For example, integrity, honor, and respect are principles that shape our behavior and how we choose to live, lead, and interact with others.

Priorities define the areas where we invest our time, talent, and treasure. They're often defined by the people who are most important to us, our God-given capacity, and the resources God has entrusted to us.

Beliefs ground us.

Principles guide us.

Priorities order us.

Together, they form the values on which we build our lives. When we fail to identify our values, our character becomes susceptible to what's most convenient at the moment. Without clear values, we create the perfect conditions for sinkholes to form within us.

Layer #2: Grow Your Character

Author Bob Goff once said, "We plant sod where God wants us to plant seed. He's more interested in growing our character than having us look finished."[26] But character doesn't grow by accident. We must embrace three practices to create the proper soil conditions for character to take root.

Cultivate Disciplines of Spirituality—God's character-growing process happens when we cooperate with His Spirit's work within us. The Holy Spirit leads us to do what's right and convicts us when we do what's wrong. When we submit to His transforming influence, we become less susceptible to sinkholes.

This is why spiritual disciplines—like prayer, Bible study, fasting, and worship—are so important. Richard Foster, author of the classic book *Celebration of Discipline*, observes the following:

> *God has given us the Disciplines of the spiritual life as a means of receiving his grace. The Disciplines allow us to place ourselves before God so that he can transform us.*[27]

> **A council of yes-men is nothing more than a one-way ticket to delusion and self-deception.**

As I noted in the last chapter, God does the transforming—not the disciplines. The disciplines are how we place ourselves before God so He can do the deep work of transformation within us. The goal is to get to *know* Christ. Becoming like Him is the byproduct. The closer we draw to Jesus, the more our character reflects integrity, generosity, and humility—qualities often compromised in leadership.

Create Boundaries of Accountability—We're all one step from stupid, and the more power we have, the less people are willing to tell us the truth. That's why we need accountability in our lives. A council of yes-men is nothing more than a one-way ticket to delusion and self-deception.

Most people think boundaries protect us from others, but the greatest boundaries protect us from ourselves. They create external structure to help us manage our internal world. They create accountability for how we behave with money, schedules, power, and relationships. Can this be painful? Perhaps! But as my friend Steve Moore observed, "Accountability, however, does not bring pain. The pain comes from the underlying problem; accountability merely exposes it."[28]

Build Circles of Community—J. R. R. Tolkien is well known for his novel *The Hobbit*.[29] The book was so successful that his publisher asked him to write a sequel. But Tolkien hit the wall every time he sat down to write. He referred to this experience as a "labor of delight" that was "transformed into a nightmare."

Tolkien could have thrown in the towel and undoubtedly felt like doing just that. But he embraced one practice that proved critical to his success: he met weekly with a small group of friends. Those friends encouraged one another, and one of them was the British writer, scholar, and lay theologian C. S. Lewis.

After the publication of Tolkien's sequel, he said of C. S. Lewis:
The unpayable debt that I owe to him was not "influence" as it is ordinarily understood, but sheer encouragement. He was for long my only audience. Only from him did I ever get the idea that my "stuff" could be more than a private hobby. But for his interest and unceasing eagerness for more I should never have brought The L. of the R. to a conclusion.[30]

The L. of the R. was *The Lord of the Rings*,[31] and it has since sold more than 150 million copies.

Leadership is hard, which is why you need a community of friends who don't care about your title or position. Without community, you'll lead from the empty tank of isolation. With community, you'll fight your battles with friends by your side. But friendships, too, require intentionality. As pastor and author Wayne Cordeiro observed:

Friends are rare these days, but it is not because they have diminished in importance. It is because we have increased in speed. Friendships are not made in the blur of life. They are made in the margins.[32]

These three practices provide the nutrient-rich soil to grow our character. Disciplines of spirituality draw us into God's presence where He can transform our hearts. Accountability gives us the external structure we need to outsmart our weaknesses. And community gives us the wisdom and encouragement to play the long game. Working together, these practices prevent the erosion that causes sinkholes to form below the surface of our hearts. As our character grows, we'll be equipped for the third layer of leading with character.

Layer #3: Model Your Behavior

Philanthropist Andrew Carnegie once said, "As I grow older, I pay less attention to what men say. I just watch what they do."[33] Modeling behavior is where you bring character to work each day. It's the public fruit of your private disciplines. Character grows inwardly, but its influence is felt outwardly.

Modeling your behavior happens when you do what you say you will do. It's behaving with integrity when you're under pressure. It's more than talking about values but actually living them out. It's asking for forgiveness when you step out of line. It's telling the truth when it's inconvenient. It's receiving feedback with grace and humility. It's showing compassion when others are hurting.

The apostle Paul implored his young apprentice Timothy to model behavior worth imitating. He said, "Don't let anyone look down on you because you are young, but set an example for the believers in speech, in conduct, in love, in faith and in purity (1 Timothy 4:12, NIV). Notice, Paul tells Timothy to model behavior in five categories of character:

- Speech (what you say)
- Conduct (how you live)
- Love (your relationship with others)
- Faith (your relationship with God)
- Purity (your morality)

These five expressions of character are what people look for when they interact with us. People don't care about our values if our behavior doesn't back them up. But when our speech, conduct, love, faith, and purity are aligned with our values, people will not only respect us, but they'll serve the organization with quiet confidence. The reason is simple—they won't fear being swallowed by a sinkhole hiding below our character.

Layer two (growing your character) and layer three (modeling your behavior) should work seamlessly together. The growing happens in private, so the modeling can happen in public.

Layer #4: Debrief Your Wisdom

Character starts *in* us, but it should ultimately extend *beyond* us. That happens when we debrief matters of character with the people we lead. That's what the apostle Paul did with Timothy.

Paul said:

But you, Timothy, certainly know what I teach, and how I live, and what my purpose in life is. You know my faith, my patience, my love, and my endurance. You know how much persecution and suffering I have endured.

> *You know all about how I was persecuted in Antioch, Iconium, and Lystra—but the Lord rescued me from all of it.* —2 Timothy 3:10-11

Paul highlighted several character traits, not to exalt himself, but to use each trait as a teachable moment with Timothy.

Whether you call it debriefing, teaching, or coaching, be sure to talk about character development with your team. The goal isn't to brag about your character or present an image of perfection. Instead, talk about the safeguards you've established in your own life to keep sinkholes from forming in your heart. Give examples of when your character was tested and how you responded. Point to moments when you failed a character test, and then humbly share the lessons you learned in the process. In addition, share tips and content from other leaders who model good values and lead with character.

These simple steps will help your team benefit from your hard-earned wisdom on character development. Of course, the key to remember is that your coaching must be backed up with character. Debriefing your wisdom without modeling your behavior will drain the moral authority out of your teaching. That brings us to the final layer of leading with character.

Layer #5: Multiply Your Example

The example we set for others has the power to multiply far beyond us. However, multiplication happens with good character *and* bad character. Let me share two startling case studies, beginning with bad character.

Case study number one: King Jeroboam.

Jeroboam became the king of Israel in 931 BC. Everything went well until Jeroboam's heart turned away from the Lord. Then, the prophet Ahijah delivered this message to the king via Jeroboam's wife:

"I promoted you from the ranks of the common people and made you ruler over my people Israel.... You have done more evil than all who lived before you." —1 Kings 14:7b, 9a

Then, Ahijah prophesied that God would abandon Israel because not only did Jeroboam sin, but he made Israel sin as well (1 Kings 14:16). That began a long decline for Israel.

From Jeroboam to Hoshea, there were nineteen kings in Israel. The reign of these nineteen kings lasted 209 years (from 931-722 BC), and each one of them did evil in the sight of the Lord. Of the eighteen kings who followed King Jeroboam, fourteen of them were described with a slight variation of the following passage: "But he did what was evil in the Lord's sight. He *followed the example of Jeroboam* son of Nebad, continuing the sins that Jeroboam had led Israel to commit."[34]

Of the remaining four kings—though Jeroboam's name isn't mentioned—Scripture describes three of them as kings who led Israel to sin or who followed the example of previous kings linked to Jeroboam's sin. One king—King Shallum—has very little description because he only reigned one month before being assassinated (2 Kings 13:15-13). This 209-year stretch closes with these words:

But Jeroboam drew Israel away from following the LORD and made them commit a great sin. And the people of Israel persisted in all the evil ways of Jeroboam. They did not turn from these sins. —2 Kings 17:21-22

This long reign of kings "followed the example of Jeroboam." For over two hundred years, the sins of nineteen kings can be traced back to one man. Jeroboam led by example—an evil example—and his corrupt character multiplied to everyone who followed him for generations to come.

Case study number two: The Apostle Paul.

Paul did the exact opposite of King Jeroboam. He multiplied good character *around* him and *beyond* him. To the believers in Corinth, he wrote:

> *Therefore I urge you to imitate me. For this reason I have sent to you Timothy, my son whom I love, who is faithful in the Lord. He will remind you of my way of life in Christ Jesus, which agrees with what I teach everywhere in every church.* —*1 Corinthians 4:16-17 (NIV)*

Paul invited others to follow his example, and he sent Timothy to teach his example to the Christians in Corinth.

In Philippians 3:17, Paul offers another example of character multiplication when he writes, "Join together in following my example, brothers and sisters, and just as you have us as a model, keep your eyes on those who live as we do" (NIV). Paul lived what he taught, and he pointed to his life—and the lives of others—as a model worth following. Around him and beyond him, Paul multiplied an example of God-honoring character and a deep commitment to the mission of Christ.

The character of two leaders—King Jeroboam and the apostle Paul—produced two very different outcomes. One exhibited character that led to a wave of destruction, and the other modeled character that inspired people toward righteousness and a legacy of spiritual fruit. In both cases, their character multiplied to future generations.

> **Your example has the power to extend to future generations, but you determine whether it will be one worth following.**

Your character will do the same.

Your character is multiplied beyond you—whether good or bad. Keep that in mind when you're leading your family. Keep that front and center when you're leading a ministry, business, or organization. Your example has the power to extend to future generations, but you determine whether it will be one worth following.

So, how do you multiply your example? Guide the people you lead through the previous four layers. Help them identify their values. Show them how to grow their character and model God-honoring behavior. Then, challenge them to debrief their character with others. When they exhibit each layer of the process, you'll add the multiplying layer to your character, and they'll be equipped to keep the multiplication process going.

LAYERS, NOT LEVELS

There's one final note I need to make about the five layers of leading with character: these are *layers* that you add, not *levels* that you leave. In other words, you don't leave one level to obtain a new level. Instead, as you progress through each layer, you pick them up and take them with you. As you build layer upon layer, you'll effectively lead with character.

To help you get started, utilize Leadership Tool #3: The 5 Layers of Character. These tools will help you do a self-assessment of the categories of character noted in 1 Timothy 4:12: speech, life, love, faith, and purity. In addition, you'll put together an action plan to maximize the five layers of leading with character.

INSANELY PRACTICAL REFLECTION AND DISCUSSION

1. Why do leaders seem to be crashing at an alarming rate, and what do you think is the cause of the acceleration?
2. What values (Level 1) have had the greatest impact on your character development?
3. What are some practical ways you could implement the three keys to grow your character (Level 2)—cultivate disciplines of spirituality, create boundaries of accountability, and build circles of community?
4. How do you (or could you) use your character to help others develop their character (Levels 3, 4, and 5)?

LEADERSHIP TOOL #3
The Five Layers of Character

First Timothy 4:12 challenges us to set an example in five areas: speech, life, love, faith, and purity. Before we can set an example, we must first assess our health—and potential sinkholes—in each area. Using the chart below, rate yourself Green, Yellow, or Red in each of the character descriptions. Green means the character trait is healthy and strong in your life. Yellow means you need to make improvements. Red means it's a clear weakness and needs immediate attention. Then, use the Practicing the 5 Layers of Character tool to take your next steps.

CHARACTER	CHARACTER TRAIT RATING		
	Green	Yellow	Red
SPEECH			
My words are consistently life-giving to others.			
I avoid foul and degrading language.			
I exhibit a positive attitude and tone.			
LIFE			
I model the fruit of the Spirit (Galatians 5).			
I lead with humility, integrity, and generosity.			
I'm not making any character compromises.			
LOVE			
Those closest to me feel loved by me.			
I love and serve those on my team.			
I exhibit love and compassion to the hurting.			
FAITH			
I live surrendered to the lordship of Christ.			
I engage daily in spiritual disciplines.			
I wisely steward my time, talent, and treasure.			

PURITY			
I live with purity in my morals and ethics.			
I have clear safeguards to protect my purity.			
I have people who hold me accountable.			

1.
2.
3.

LAYER #1: IDENTIFY YOUR VALUES
List 3-6 values below that you endeavor to live and lead by each day.

LAYER #2: GROW YOUR CHARACTER
Rate yourself in the following areas on a scale of 1 to 5 (5 being the best).

Rating Area	1	2	3	4	5
I regularly practice disciplines of spirituality.					
I have clear boundaries of accountability.					
I'm doing life with a supportive community.					

My Action Plan to Grow My Character:

LAYER #3: MODEL YOUR BEHAVIOR

Describe one step you'll take to model good behavior in each of the following traits:

Speech	Life	Love	Faith	Purity

LAYER #4: DEBRIEF YOUR WISDOM

Describe your plan to debrief matters of character with others.

LAYER #5: MULTIPLY YOUR EXAMPLE

What steps will you take to help your team add each layer to their character?

Download the Character Assessment and Practicing the 5 Layers of Character at insanelypracticalleadership.com.

CHAPTER 4

HOW TO THINK LIKE A LEADER

"In a very real sense, my world begins and ends between my ears. I don't have to be brain-dead to be brain-defeated."
—**Mark Batterson and Richard Foth**

In our years of leadership, Karen and I have faced our share of challenges, disappointments, and unexpected ridicule.

Once, an angry church member dragged our names through the mud on social media. The long rant was filled with complaints about why we didn't care and our total lack of compassion during their time of need. Paragraph after paragraph, they cast blame and poured out grievances. Of course, there was no mention of the phone calls we had made, the prayers we had offered, or our attempts to help.

But then it got *really* personal.

It wasn't enough to tell us how little we cared, so they employed tactics like body shaming and bullying to lambast us and our close friends. We used self-restraint, refusing to get sucked into the accusatory mayhem. Instead, we tried to make contact to address their concerns, but to no avail. We finally had to report the post to Facebook, and in a relatively short time, they removed it.

There are also unique challenges to pastoring in an urban context. We serve a highly transient population, many of whom are educated young professionals. We love investing in these aspiring young leaders. They're hungry to grow and willing to serve, and we see the powerful work God is doing in their lives. But we've also become accustomed to the reality that job transfers and higher education pursuits will eventually move many of them on to other cities. Having a "sending" mindset is essential, or you'll quickly become discouraged.

On top of that, we're located in a twelve-block area with twenty bars. In the last few years, 17 percent of the city's alcohol permits have been issued in the zip code where we're located.[35] And on weekend nights, up to ten thousand patrons fill the bars and the streets.[36] The police presence is high when the sun goes down, and there's a constant effort by the city to try to keep the area safe.

Because of the party scene on Saturday nights, we never know what we'll find on Sunday mornings. We've discovered car bumpers on the sidewalk from apparent wrecks the night before. Beer cans, a lady's bikini, and invite cards to strip joints have been strewn along the side of the building. Partiers have puked on the sidewalk near our front door, not to mention in the parking lot. Once, someone grabbed a cast iron sidewalk water cover and chucked it through our window. On another occasion, a car hit a bus stop sign, bent it across the sidewalk, slamming it into our window. Thankfully, the tint on the window kept it from shattering into a million pieces.

These inconveniences don't just occur outside our building; they happen inside too. We once launched a major building renovation that required the installation of a fire sprinkler system. When the crew tested the system, a stream of water shot out of a pipe and landed perfectly on our sound board, light board, and computer. The work crew had failed to cap the pipe in the auditorium ceiling. And, of course, I just happened to be giving another pastor in our community a tour of the building when it happened. I stood there in disbelief, ready to give somebody an unholy piece of my mind. Meanwhile, silent songs of praise welled up in our worship pastor's heart as visions of a new soundboard filled his mind.

WHAT'S YOUR BIGGEST PROBLEM?

There's no such thing as a problem-free leader. Leadership isn't for the faint of heart, and whether you asked for it or not, most days will greet you with a new problem to solve or tension to resolve.

What about you?

What's your *biggest problem* as a leader?

An empty bank account? A failed product launch? Declining growth? Abysmal fourth-quarter sales?

Or maybe your biggest problem isn't a "what" but a "who." A coworker out to get you. A manager gone rogue. A disgruntled customer. A divisive parishioner.

Or perhaps your biggest problem sounds more like a "when." When will the marketing plan work? When will the bill come due? When will the next staff member resign? When will the other shoe drop?

> **Your biggest problem—and my biggest problem—is how we think.**

Leadership abounds with problems. But the longer I've led, the more I've come to realize our biggest problem is not a lack of money, declining growth, or a disgruntled customer. The biggest mountain before us isn't a lack of opportunity, a scathing review, or even an unexpected crisis. I'm not suggesting these aren't problems—nor am I trying to minimize them—I'm simply saying these aren't our *biggest* problems. Instead, *your* biggest problem—and *my* biggest problem—is how we think.

More than anything else, how we think defines who we are, how high we climb, and how well we lead. Poverty of the mind not only precedes poverty of our circumstances, but it also precedes poverty of our leadership. Authors Mark Batterson and Richard Foth noted, "In a very real sense, my world begins and ends between my ears. I don't have to be brain-dead to be brain-defeated."[37] If we don't change how we think, our life and leadership will never grow beyond where we are right now.

HOW TO THINK LIKE A LEADER

The most effective leaders *think like leaders*. That sounds obvious and redundant, so let me say it another way: leadership isn't just an action; it's a mindset. If we don't lead ourselves to think like leaders, our limiting beliefs will become our ceiling. The best leaders silence the negative self-talk and cultivate eight insanely practical mindsets.

1) Leaders Think Confidence vs. Self-Doubt

I'm a "thinker" by nature, and I like answers to my questions before I jump into a new initiative. But if I'm not careful, I'll overthink an issue, considering the endless litany of options available to me before I take my first step. While this is helpful when I'm making important decisions, I can also second-guess myself. That's when self-doubt speaks the loudest, and my confidence can leak.

Author and leadership coach Dan Reiland said:

A lack of confidence can cause you to hold back, become indecisive, and communicate without enough authority. Being underconfident is believing less in your own ability than God does, and less in what God can do in and through you.[38]

On the other hand, confidence is the courage-booster of leadership. It gives you the inner resolve to step into uncertainty and act in the face of fear. So, how do you put a muzzle on self-doubt and bolster your confidence? It starts with three foundational keys.

Ground Your Identity. The self-talk of negativity, disapproval, and self-doubt will become the narrator of your life if you don't ground your identity in Christ. Before Jesus began his ministry or performed a single miracle, His heavenly Father declared, "This is my Son, whom I love; with him I am well pleased" (Matthew 3:17, NIV). Jesus knew who He was and whose He was, and that identity fueled his life and leadership. We, too, must ground our identity in Christ and the good things He declares about us. At a recent pastor's retreat, I heard author Scott Wilson say, "You will not consistently act in a way that's inconsistent with how you gain self-worth." Jesus is the Divine Source from whom we gain our self-worth.

Increase Your Clarity. A lack of confidence shows up when we incessantly second-guess our decisions. Vacillating in a constant mode of what ifs and what abouts gives self-doubt undue authority over our lives. How do you overcome it? Increase your clarity about the situation around you and the decisions before you. When clarity increases, confidence quickly follows. Chapter 6 will sharpen your clarity with ten keys to good decision-making.

Grow Your Competency. Self-doubt abounds when you find yourself in situations that exceed your competency. When you're in over your head, confidence craters to an all-time low. That's why expanding your knowledge, growing your skills, and acquiring deeper levels of experience are so important. They grow your competence, so you can tackle your toughest leadership challenges.

Identity, clarity, and competency are the antidote to a self-doubt mindset and the recipe for bold confidence. Identity grounds you, clarity elevates you, and competency advances you. Together, they boost your confidence to see and seize the future.

2) Leaders Think Possibilities vs. Excuses

Over the years, Career Builder has published some bizarre excuses people give for being late to work. Some of their real-life excuses include:

- My deodorant was frozen to the windowsill.
- My car door fell off.
- I dreamt I was already at work.
- I had an early morning gig as a clown.
- My fake eyelashes were stuck together.
- I was here, but I fell asleep in the parking lot.
- Although it has been five years, I forgot I did not work at my former employer's location and drove there by accident.[39]

Those are some creative excuses. Unfortunately, leaders also come up with excuses, and Moses is a perfect example. When God called him to return to Egypt and lead His people out of slavery, Moses tried to dodge God's call with five excuses.

Excuse #1: *Insignificance: I'm Not Important Enough*—God told Moses to go to Egypt and deliver the Israelites out of slavery, but Moses responded, "Who am I to appear before Pharaoh? Who am I to lead the people of Israel out of Egypt?" (Exodus 3:11). Moses felt insignificant for the task. He told God, "I'm a nobody! Why would you pick me?"

Excuse #2: *Incompetence: I Don't Know Enough*—Moses began protesting with another excuse. He said, "If I go to the people of Israel and tell them, 'The God of your ancestors has sent me to you,' they will ask me, 'What is his name?' Then what should I tell them?" (Exodus 3:13). Moses didn't have the answers to move forward. For him, his competence didn't cut it.

Excuse #3: *Invalid: I'm Not Credible Enough*—Moses pulled another excuse out of his bag of insecurities: "What if they won't believe me or listen to me? What if they say, 'The LORD never appeared to you'?" (Exodus 4:1). Moses doubted his credibility. He had already blown it once, and he figured the Israelites would point out his credibility gap if he tried to come to their rescue a second time.

Excuse #4: *Inadequacy: I'm Not Skilled Enough*—After three failed excuses, Moses reminded God of his speech impediment: "O LORD, I'm not very good with words. I never have been, and I'm not now, even though you have spoken to me. I get tongue-tied, and my words get tangled" (Exodus 4:10).

Interpretation: "God, I'm inadequate for the job. My skills don't measure up."

Excuse #5: *Inferior: I'm Not Good Enough*—Moses tops off his excuses with one last plea: "Lord, please! Send anyone else" (Exodus 4:13). Exasperated by God's plan, Moses bemoans, "God, if you lined up a hundred other people, I'd be the least qualified. I'm inferior to everyone else. Please, pick someone else for this assignment."

> **Excuses are the permanent exit ramps from the highway of obedience.**

Do any of these excuses sound familiar? Perhaps you've used them a time or two to try to convince God of why you're a less-than-optimal candidate for the job. I know I have. Here's the problem: excuses are the permanent exit ramps from the highway of obedience. Excuses are an attempt to acquire short-term relief from our fears and failures. But excuses always lead to the same place: regret.

That's not how good leaders think. The most effective leaders think in the realm of *possibility*. Why? Because that's where God resides. He's not weak, scrawny, pathetic, fragile, and spineless. He's all-knowing and all-powerful. That's why He didn't put up with a single excuse Moses threw at Him. Instead, God told Moses, "I've sent you" (Exodus 3:14), "I've equipped you" (Exodus 4:2), and "I'm with you" (Exodus 4:12).

3) Leaders Think Abundance vs. Scarcity

When my wife was a child, her parents took her and her brother to a pizza restaurant one evening for dinner. When the pizza was delivered to their table, Karen did a quick calculation of how many slices were in the pie compared to the number of people sitting around the table. *I have to move fast,* she thought, *if I'm going to get my fair share of pizza.* Her parents knew what she was thinking and quickly stepped in with an important life lesson: "There are plenty of ingredients in the kitchen to make another pizza." That night, Karen learned the value of an abundance mindset vs. a scarcity mindset.

An abundance mindset believes there's plenty to go around, and there will always be more. A scarcity mindset believes resources are limited, and therefore, I must grab what's mine before somebody else takes it.

We see both mindsets in action when Moses sent twelve men to spy out the land God promised to give the Israelites. When the spies returned with their report, Joshua and Caleb said, "We should go up and take possession of the land, for we can certainly do it" (Numbers 13:30, NIV). Their faith-filled confidence revealed an abundance mindset.

But the remaining ten spies came with a different report:

"We can't go up against them! They are stronger than we are!" So they spread this bad report about the land among the Israelites: "The land we traveled through and explored will devour anyone who goes to live there. All the people we saw were huge. We even saw giants there, the descendants of Anak. Next to them we felt like grasshoppers, and that's what they thought, too!" —Numbers 13:31-33

Author Dharius Daniels made a powerful observation about this passage at a conference I attended in Houston, Texas: "The spies' biggest problem wasn't the giants in the land but the grasshopper in their head." The giants in the land didn't have to do anything to defeat the spies because the grasshopper in their heads already did.

As a leader, you must understand two truths about mindset. First, your mindset is *contagious*. How you think influences the people you lead. The scarcity mindset of the ten spies infected millions of Israelites. Second, your mindset has consequences. The Israelites began crying when they heard the negative report, longing to return to Egypt. What was the ultimate consequence? They spent forty years wandering in the wilderness.

> **You have a choice to make: evict the scarcity grasshopper from your thinking or surrender your future to its control.**

Here's the craziest part of the story: the Israelites feared the very people who feared them.

If you fast forward forty years, God commands Joshua to cross the Jordan River and take the land of Canaan. Before Joshua proceeds, he sends two spies to scope out the land. In the process, these two spies meet a prostitute named Rahab who shares with them this sobering truth:

"I know the LORD has given you this land," she told them. "We are all afraid of you. Everyone in the land is living in terror. For we have heard how the LORD made a dry path for you through the Red Sea when you left Egypt. And we know what you did to Sihon and Og, the two Amorite kings east of the Jordan River, whose people you completely destroyed. No wonder our hearts have melted in fear! No one has the courage to fight after hearing such things. For the LORD your God is the supreme God of the heavens above and the earth below." —Joshua 2:9-11

I can only imagine what these two spies thought at that moment: *Do you mean to tell me we've been scared for forty years when all along these people were scared of us?* I don't think I'd have done the happy dance at that moment. I'm guessing they didn't either.

You have a choice to make: evict the scarcity grasshopper from your thinking or surrender your future to its control. You can succumb to the fear of scarcity or rise with the faith of an abundance mindset. Here's the difference between the two.

Scarcity Mindset	Abundance Mindset
Focuses on lack	Focuses on God's unlimited supply
Complains about what it doesn't have	Gives thanks for what it does have
Settles for its current reality	Sees future possibilities
Is driven by fear	Is driven by faith
Hoards knowledge and resources	Freely shares knowledge and resources
Wants all the credit	Shares the credit with others
Avoids risk at all costs	Sees risk as necessary to move forward
Resents the success of others	Celebrates the success of others

Don't give scarcity the keys to your thinking. There are plenty of ingredients in the kitchen. The apostle Paul reminds us, "With God's power working in us, God can do much, much more than anything we can ask or imagine" (Ephesians 3:20, NCV). Paul refused to limit God, and so should you. Think abundance, believing Him for the "much, much more."

4) Leaders Think Innovation vs. Conformity

Innovation sounds well and good when you have nothing to lose, but once you create something successful, it's more comfortable to shift your thinking into a protective mode of conformity. Rather than continuing to create, we turn yesterday's innovation into an idol. Then, when somebody else begins to innovate, we climb our ivory tower and start throwing stones at the newest idea. R. T. Kendall captured it best when he said, "The greatest opposition to what God is doing today comes from those who were on the cutting edge of what God was doing yesterday."[40]

For that reason, innovation begins by bringing our assumptions under the microscope. Failure to do so will kill the organization's growth. This is the outcome Matthew S. Olson, Derek van Bever, and Seth Verry discovered. In a *Harvard Review* article, they write that one culprit of stalled organizational growth is "management's failure to bring the underlying assumptions that drive company strategy into line with changes in the external environment—whether because of a lack of awareness that the gap existed or was widening, or because of faulty prioritization." They went on to reveal a disturbing reality: "The assumptions the team has held the longest or the most deeply are the likeliest to be its undoing."[41]

While comfortable assumptions seem innocent enough, they're actually the enemy of growth and innovation. They drive us toward conformity and away from the lifeblood of best practices and God-inspired ideas.

To keep your organization from slipping into irrelevance, embrace the discipline of innovative thinking and resist the lure of conformity. As author Brad Lomenick once said, "When you innovate, don't idolize or your most imaginative ventures will cannibalize your creativity."[42]

Where should you start? You must welcome feedback from *external coaches* and *internal team members*. Invite external coaches to help you see with new eyes. And create a safe space for internal team members to share fresh perspectives and best practices.

To lead implies change, and visionary leaders don't possess visions of sameness. They dream of forward progress and bringing about positive change. Leaders *create* rather than *conform*. The moment you lose your innovative edge is the moment your thinking will begin to fossilize. When this happens, Olson, Bever, and Verry observe that most organizations will actually accelerate into a stall because few leaders see it coming.[43]

5) Leaders Think People vs. Programs

Industrialist and philanthropist Andrew Carnegie once said, "Take away my people but leave my factories and soon grass will grow on the factory floor. Take away my factories and leave my people and soon we will have a new and better factory."[44] Leadership is about the people, not the programs, products, or property. You design programs, but you develop people. You create products, but you cultivate people. You buy property, but you build people. When you stop developing, cultivating, and building people, the day will come when you have no more programs, products, or property.

> **When you think of people first, you won't have to worry about products and programs because the people will think of them for you.**

Leaders often tout, "Our people are our greatest asset." But are they? Really? If you made that statement in your next speech, would your employees nod their heads in agreement? Or would they roll their eyes and grumble about how they're nothing more than cogs in your wheel to create products and programs? When you think of *people first*, you won't have to worry about products and programs because the people will think of them for you.

6) Leaders Think Developing vs. Doing

Several years ago, I was invited to attend a gathering with a small group of pastors. The guest that day was Greg Surratt, the founding pastor of Seacoast Church and the president and cofounder of the Association of Related Churches (ARC). That day, Greg said something that I've never forgotten. He told us, "There's too much ministry to be done to hire people to do ministry. You have to hire people who have the ability to get ministry done through others." His point was simply that pastors must be developers of people rather than merely doers of ministry. When we help people discover and deploy their gifts and abilities, ministry multiplies far beyond our own capacity.

> **The greatest fruit you'll ever produce is the people you develop.**

Unfortunately, today, we often equate high achievers with being high-capacity leaders. That's not always the case. Just because you get an enormous amount of work done doesn't mean you're a great leader. It simply means you have a strong work ethic and know how to manage your time. Leaders are separated from high achievers by their ability to develop people. High achievers are *doers*. Leaders are *developers*. One focuses on *doing tasks* and the other focuses on *developing people*. The greatest fruit you'll ever produce is the people you develop.

People vs. Programs and *Developing vs. Doing* separate leaders from managers. Leadership is future-oriented, but management is fixed on today. Leadership is people-focused, but management is systems-focused. Leaders dream of the possibilities, but managers plan the details. Leadership is effective, but management is efficient. You need both—leaders and managers—but your thinking must change if you're going to start leading.

7) Leaders Think Empowerment vs. Control

Author and pastor Craig Groeschel says, "You can have control or you can have growth, but you can't have both."[45] Leaders want growth, so they deliberately give up control and empower the people they lead. Yes, this feels risky. And yes, this stresses out control freaks, like me. But if you're going to think like a leader, you must empower people with power. That's the only way to effectively lead.

Navy Captain D. Michael Abrashoff said, "Empowering means defining the parameters in which people are allowed to operate, and then setting them free."[46] If you fail to do this, people will rely on you to make all their decisions for them. Abrashoff makes it clear: "If all you give are orders, then all you'll get are order-takers."[47]

Empowerment requires two keys: *responsibility* and *authority*. You must first release responsibility to other members of your team, then let go of the authority that goes with it. If people still need you to make all the decisions about the responsibility you've given to them, then you haven't fully empowered your team. Responsibility and authority are the two tracks that the train of empowerment runs on.

8) Leaders Think Long-Term vs. Short-Term

My dad and mom weren't wealthy, and opulent luxury was never their standard of living. But throughout their lives, they always exercised incredible financial discipline.

Growing up, both of their parents were poor, and neither of them enjoyed special perks or superior privileges. Mom was born and raised in England, and Dad's parents emigrated from Italy to Rochester, New York, where he was born. However, Dad wanted a better life, so in his early twenties, he joined the Air Force, and after twenty-six years of service, he went to work for the United States Postal Service.

Dad recently passed away at the age of ninety-five. He and Mom were married for fifty-nine years. And while they weren't wealthy, they somehow managed to pay off their house early, avoid credit card debt, prepare for retirement, buy each child their first car, and put four kids through college debt-free. I'll be forever grateful for their sacrifice.

How does this happen?

How do two people from poor families build a life together, create a secure retirement, and make it possible for their kids to graduate college without a giant loan hanging over their heads? It's certainly not because Dad's Air Force and Postal Service paychecks were exorbitant. And it's not because Mom worked for a high-powered Fortune 100 company—because she didn't. For the most part, she has been a stay-at-home mom who worked a few hours a week at a local department store.

Mom and Dad's secret wasn't the size of their paychecks.

And there was no surprise inheritance or lucky lotto number that pushed them over the top.

Instead, their superpower was *long-term perspective*.

Harvard University sociologist Dr. Edward Banfield did extensive research on what allows people to become financially independent. Most people would attribute financial independence to good fortune, education, race, family background, intelligence, or social connections. But what Dr. Banfield learned surprised him. The biggest predictor of financial success is "long time perspective." In other words, people who became financially successful made today's decisions with tomorrow in mind.[48]

> **The problem with short-term thinking is that it usually undermines long-term results.**

That same long-term perspective not only works with finances but also in leadership. Today, we have an epidemic of leaders who think short-term. Politicians make short-term promises, so they can get re-elected. Business leaders make short-term decisions, so they'll see a bump in this quarter's sales. The problem with short-term thinking is that it usually undermines long-term results. It pursues quick fixes and temporary satisfaction at the expense of tomorrow's well-being.

To be a mature leader, you must think and act differently. Embrace a long-term perspective, and then courageously do what's right *today* for the long-term good of the organization. This isn't a popular mindset, but it's essential if you want to make an impact that extends beyond your lifetime.

These eight mindsets reveal how good leaders think. To master the art of leading yourself, you must master your thinking. To help you get started, use Leadership Tool #4: Leader Think. This tool will help you think confidence, abundance, possibilities, innovation, people, development, empowerment, and long-term. After all, how you think determines the future you create.

INSANELY PRACTICAL REFLECTION AND DISCUSSION

1. Just because you have a leadership position doesn't mean you automatically think like a leader. How have you found this to be true?
2. What "grasshopper" in your head taunts you the most, and how do you deal with its tormenting lies?
3. Which of the eight mindsets is your greatest strength, and which one is your biggest weakness?
4. What's the first step you need to take to begin thinking more like a leader?

LEADERSHIP TOOL #4
Leader Think

To identify gaps in your ability to think like a leader, use the tool below to rate yourself in each area on a scale from 1 to 5 (5 being the best). After completing the assessment, answer the question below.

LEADERS THINK...	1	2	3	4	5
CONFIDENCE VS. SELF-DOUBT					
My identity is firmly grounded in Christ.					
I make confident decisions and don't second-guess myself.					
I am confident in my calling, abilities, and vision.					
ABUNDANCE VS. SCARCITY					
I regularly give thanks rather than complaining.					
I celebrate others' success rather than resenting it.					
I lead with faith rather than fear.					
POSSIBILITIES VS. EXCUSES					
I see opportunities rather than obstacles.					
I take responsibility rather than making excuses.					
I believe I'm qualified rather than inferior to do the job.					
INNOVATION VS. CONFORMITY					
I willingly let go of the past to embrace fresh innovation.					
I challenge long-held assumptions to pursue better ideas.					
I actively seek outside perspective to remain relevant.					
PEOPLE VS. PROGRAMS					
I consistently put people before programs and strategies.					
I show value to people more than allegiance to my ideas.					
The people I lead feel known and noticed by me.					
DEVELOPING VS. DOING					
I'm more focused on developing people than doing tasks.					
I allocate a significant amount of time to mentor others.					
I focus on vision and people more than systems and efficiency.					

EMPOWERMENT VS. CONTROL				
I'm careful not to control or micromanage people.				
I willingly and regularly empower people with power.				
I delegate responsibility AND decision-making authority.				
LONG-TERM VS. SHORT-TERM				
I avoid short-term fixes for long-term health.				
I maintain good perspective in the face of real problems.				
I make hard decisions when unpopular in the short-term.				

In which two areas do you need to begin thinking more like a leader, and what steps will you take to improve?

Download the Leader Think tool at insanelypracticalleadership.com.

CHAPTER 5

HOW TO MANAGE YOUR TIME

"You have to decide what your highest priorities are and have the courage—pleasantly, smilingly, unapologetically—to say no to other things. And the way you do that is by having a bigger 'yes' burning inside."
—Stephen R. Covey

Several years ago, a friend of mine worked in a fast-paced, high-stress business environment. He carried big responsibilities and faced high demands, not to mention long hours and a toxic culture. Every day felt like a pressure cooker, and he never knew if he was going to get burned.

In short, my friend hated his job.

Every time I'd see him, I asked, "How's it going?" His answer was always the same: "Busy." His one-word answer was all he could muster to spare me the bedlam.

But then his situation changed.

He got another job—a much *better* job.

He had a great boss, and he loved the organization's mission. The team, the pay, and the culture were great. It was the opposite of his former workplace, and he *loved* it.

But I noticed something interesting. When I'd ask my usual question, "How's it going?" his answer remained the same: "Busy."

His answer wasn't "awesome," or "great" or "amazing." He didn't rave about how much better work was—even though it *was*. He was just, "Busy."

"Busy" is the one-word answer many of us give for our lives. We wear "busy" like a badge of honor. After all, who wants to be labeled as a lazy slug or an idle sloth? We'd much rather tout our busyness as a strong work ethic, a commitment to excellence, or a desire to make a difference. We're "busy" for all the right reasons.

Or are we?

THE CURRENCY OF TIME

Time is our most precious currency. We make purchases each day with the currency of time. The right use of your time can purchase outstanding results at work or an "A" in your business class. The right use of your time can even purchase a closer friendship, a healthier marriage, or a deeper faith in God.

On the other hand, the wrong use of your time can purchase a pink slip from your employer. The wrong use of your time can purchase strained family relationships, habits of laziness, an addiction to video games, an "F" in your business class, or a nonexistent relationship with God.

The right purchases deliver the right outcomes. The wrong purchases bankrupt your productivity, relationships, and life. We can spend time *frivolously* or invest it *wisely*; either way, how we use our time reveals what we value most.

So, how valuable is *your* time?

In his book *Becoming a Coaching Leader*,[49] Daniel Harkavy offers a great perspective on determining the value of your time. He suggests that you start by identifying your desired annual income five years from now. Maybe you want to double your income. Perhaps you want to start a business and increase your earning potential. Regardless of your plan, pick a number.

Then, open the calculator on your phone and divide your desired annual income by 2,080. That's how many hours there are in a forty-hour workweek during an entire year. Once you divide your desired income by 2,080, you'll come up with an hourly rate. For example, if you want to earn $100,000 per year and you divide it by 2,080, you'll make about $48 per hour. If you want to earn $250,000 per year, you'll make approximately $120 per hour. You get the idea.

Now, look at that hourly dollar amount on your calculator and ask yourself this question: *Is how I currently use each hour of my day worth that much money?*

You might push back and say, "Stephen, I don't make that much money per hour." I get it, but that's not my question. The question is, *Is how I CURRENTLY use each hour of my day worth that much money?*

Let's make it personal.

Is scrolling through social media worth $48 an hour to you? Is watching TV for three or four hours each night worth $120 an hour to you? Is spending excessive hours on your favorite hobby worth the number on your calculator right now? Take how you *currently* use your time and ask yourself if it's worth the amount of money you hope to make in five years.

If your answer is "No," I have news for you: if you don't change how you use your time today, you won't earn your desired income tomorrow. Today's changes deliver tomorrow's outcomes.

This example doesn't encompass the full value of time, but it does help us see time in a new light. Time is a precious resource. How you invest time determines the habits you develop, the person you become, and the difference you make. And time doesn't just matter to you; it also matters to God.

TWO TRUTHS ABOUT TIME

Time is a resource entrusted to us by God. We can't manufacture more time; we can only steward it, and a closer look at Scripture shows us how to steward time in two important ways.

First, time is a resource to steward *spiritually*. Ephesians 5:11 says, "Don't waste your time on useless work, mere busywork, the barren pursuits of darkness" (MSG). The apostle Paul goes on to describe "barren pursuits of darkness" as sexual immorality, greed, and obscene talk. His point is clear: don't waste your time on unhealthy and unholy pursuits.

Second, time is a resource to steward *wisely*. Proverbs 21:5 says, "Good planning and hard work lead to prosperity, but hasty shortcuts lead to poverty." Inherent in this verse is the wise stewardship of time. Good planning doesn't happen in a flash, and hard work is a matter of working *smart*, not just working *hard*. Then, there's Psalm 90:12: "Teach us to realize the brevity of life, so that we may grow in wisdom," and Hebrews 9:27, "Everyone must die once, and after that be judged by God" (GNT). When you realize the brevity of life, you begin to see time as a precious resource entrusted to you by God. And when you realize that at the end of your life, you will stand before God, it compels you to steward your life (and your time) in a way that matters for eternity.

HOW TO MANAGE YOUR TIME

Most time management methods focus on getting more done in less time. In other words, it's about employing tips and tricks, tools and tactics, to squeeze more productivity out of every minute. That's an important part of time management, but it's incomplete. Insanely practical time management is much more holistic in its approach. It functions at the highest level in the sweet spot of three overlapping circles.

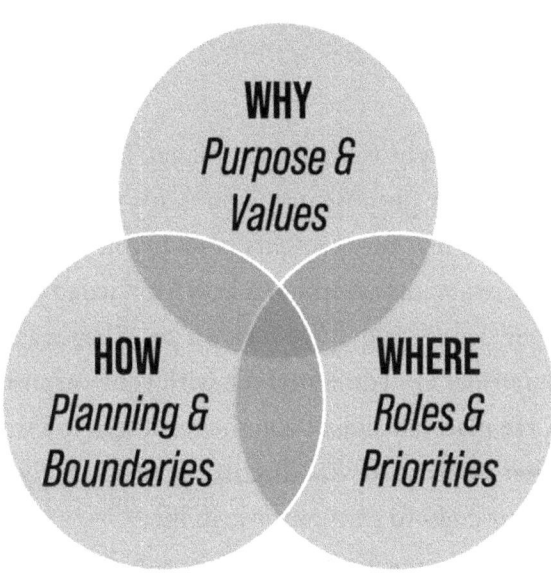

CIRCLE #1: WHY: Purpose and Values

Time management doesn't start with time. It starts with your *purpose* and *values*. Without a well-defined purpose and clearly stated values, you'll efficiently manage your time to accomplish the wrong things. That's not a picture of success, much less significance. Who cares if you get the wrong things done quicker? Purpose and values are the North Star of time management. They are the "why" that helps you answer the question, *Does what I'm getting done even matter?*

> **If you discover your God-given design, you'll discover clues to your purpose in life.**

Purpose defines why you're on the planet. I unpack the process of discovering your purpose in my book *Do Good Works*,[50] so let me summarize a few key thoughts here. If you want to discover your purpose, you must understand how God wired you. In other words, rather than asking, *What is my purpose?* begin asking, *How did God design me?* God designed you with your purpose in mind; therefore, He placed inside of you the resources you would need to fulfill that purpose. If you discover your God-given design, you'll discover clues to your purpose in life.

Some of your unique traits are your *personality, natural talents,* and *passions*. In addition, over time, you've acquired *skills*, gained *experience*, and expanded your *knowledge*. And if you're a follower of Christ, God has also deposited *spiritual gifts* within you. He may have even *called* you to a specific task, role, or mission.

Each of these traits is like a puzzle piece. When we put a puzzle together, we usually organize the pieces into colors and themes. We group together the pieces that look like sky, trees, or flowers. We find the edges, so we can quickly connect them. This is an important part of assembling a puzzle, but it's not the starting point. Before looking for patterns and themes, we *first* turn all the puzzle pieces face up.

The same is true with your life purpose puzzle. You start by turning the puzzle pieces that describe your life face-up—personality, talents, passions, skills, experience, knowledge, spiritual gifts, and calling. Then, you identify patterns and themes in how God designed you. Once these puzzle pieces come into focus, your next step is to carefully hone them into a life mission statement. To do this, ask yourself three helpful questions:

- **ACTION:** *What has God equipped me to do?* This question is answered by looking at your personality, talents, skills, knowledge, and spiritual gifts. These puzzle pieces reveal what you are most gifted to do. They are the action part of your life mission statement.
- **AUDIENCE:** *Who is God leading me to serve?* Your life mission should benefit somebody besides just yourself. Your passions, experience, and calling will help you identify the audience God has called you to serve. In other words, your audience is whom you serve with your actions.
- **OUTCOME:** *What outcomes do I desire to see in my audience?* Your passions and calling will help you identify the outcomes (or results) you want your audience to experience.

Simply put, when you do your actions for your audience, it should result in specific outcomes.

Here's an example of my life mission statement that answers the three questions above: "My life mission is to lead, coach, and equip *(ACTION)* leaders and churches *(AUDIENCE)* to engage in the process of personal growth, develop their full leadership capacity, and produce effective, Kingdom-advancing ministry *(OUTCOME)*." My life mission statement answers all three questions (Action, Audience, and Outcome), and my life purpose puzzle pieces inform each question.

By identifying my purpose, I've established a clear vision of success. With that vision in focus, I can allocate my time to fulfill it. But first I must identify the second part of "Why"—my values.

Values are the constant people, principles, and priorities that guide our lives. They're the internal rules of the game that influence our behavior, what we do, and how we spend our time and money. Clear values reveal what matters most. To help you identify your values, answer these questions:

- **PEOPLE:** *Who is more important to me than anyone else?* Examples of those whom you value might include God, your spouse, kids, friends, or coworkers. We spend time with them more than anyone else.
- **PRINCIPLES:** *What principles do I stand for above all others?* Examples of principles are integrity, excellence, compassion, teamwork, and the Golden Rule. These principles shape how we behave.
- **PRIORITIES:** *What is most important to you?* Examples of priorities include faith, work, personal growth, fitness, fun,

volunteerism, and community. These priorities influence what we do.

Your answers to these questions will give you a quick snapshot of whom and what you value most. Once you make a list, narrow it down to five to seven core values.

Again, your *purpose* and *values* define the "Why" of time management. They define which game you are playing and the rules you are playing by.

CIRCLE #2: WHERE: Roles and Priorities

After identifying the "Why" circle, you need to choose the *roles* and *priorities* that will help you fulfill your purpose and values. Roles and priorities are "Where" you'll invest your time.

Roles are the specific places where you can live out your purpose and values. Everybody has a variety of roles in life, such as spouse, parent, son, daughter, grandparent, volunteer, teacher, board member, student, coach, manager, employee, team member, artist, salesman, or hundreds of other roles.

Each role is unique and comes with the opportunity to make a difference. The question is, which roles will help you fulfill your purpose and live out your values? They may be roles you currently hold or new roles you want to pursue. In general, roles fall into five categories:
- **Community**—A role in your family, community, city, or country
- **Campus**—A role in a school, college, or university
- **Church**—A role in your local church
- **Career**—A role at work or in a specific industry

- **Culture**—A role in a stream of culture (business, education, government, healthcare, arts, media, entertainment, the social sector, religion, family, etc.)

Don't worry so much about where a role fits, as some roles will fit in multiple categories. Instead, use the list above to help you identify the roles where your purpose and values can be lived out each day.

Priorities are the most important responsibilities in each of your roles. Some leaders prioritize their schedules, but the most effective leaders schedule their priorities. This starts by identifying the priorities that will deliver the greatest impact in each of your roles.

John Maxwell observed that you can't manage time. It's static. You can't add to it or take away from it. But what you *can* do is identify your most important priorities with three helpful questions:

- What is required of me?
- What activities give me the greatest return?
- What activities give me the greatest reward?

When you answer the three "Rs" (required, return, and reward) for each of your roles, you will discover your highest priorities in those roles. Where the three "Rs" overlap, you will discover how to make your most fulfilling contribution in that role. And, of course, you want your "Rs" to line up with the way God designed you.[51]

Another helpful way to focus on your highest priorities is to practice the 80/20 rule, which says 20 percent of your activities will deliver 80 percent of your results. In other words, if you have ten tasks to do, two of them will deliver 80 percent of the impact. The other eight tasks are low-return activities. You may need to outsource or delegate them to someone else, or you may need to stop doing them altogether. Rather than wasting your time on the 80 percent, begin allocating as much time as possible to the top 20 percent of your priorities. These are the highest priorities that will produce your greatest return.

> **Urgency is reactive, but the important is proactive.**

Stephen R. Covey said, "You have to decide what your highest priorities are and have the courage—pleasantly, smilingly, unapologetically—to say no to other things. And the way you do that is by having a bigger 'yes' burning inside."[52] Your priorities—aligned with your purpose, values, and roles—are your "bigger yes." You must resist the constant lure to abandon the important for the urgent. Urgency is *reactive*, but the important is *proactive*.

CIRCLE #3: HOW: Planning and Boundaries

When you define your "Why" (Purpose and Values), you'll be equipped to choose your "Where" (Roles and Priorities). Once you've established clear priorities for each role, you must then engage the third circle—"How." "How" keeps your priorities in focus with two important practices: *planning* and *boundaries*.

Planning creates a system to maximize the minutes of your day. Much of the time management advice available today is focused on planning your time. While there are hundreds of tips and tricks to time management, let me share five foundational practices.

- **Select the Right Tool**—There are plenty of time management tools on the market. Whether it's computer software, a mobile app, or a paper planner, find a tool that works for you. The right tool will be proficient, work with your personality, and help you focus on your priorities. Most importantly, the right tool is the one you'll actually use.
- **Conduct a Weekly Meeting with Yourself**—At the beginning of each week, set aside thirty minutes to meet with yourself. In this meeting, reflect on your goals for the quarter, what you accomplished in the previous week, and the most important priorities for the week ahead.
- **Establish Your Big Three**—Author and productivity expert Michael Hyatt advocates identifying your weekly big three and your daily big three.[53] In your meeting with yourself, identify the three most important priorities you must get done this week. As often as possible, your weekly big three should be connected to your quarterly goals. Then, each day, identify your daily big three goals. Your daily big three should help you fulfill your weekly big three. This simple strategy is how your quarterly goals and highest priorities get integrated into your daily schedule. When you establish your weekly and daily big three, they create alignment between your direction and your action.
- **Eliminate, Automate, and Delegate**—Time is precious, but so often, we use it to do tasks that we should eliminate,

automate, or delegate. How do you put these practices to work?

First, identify what you can eliminate. Do a review of your previous month's to-do list and identify the items that were a waste of time. Examples of these unnecessary tasks are mindless social media scrolling, meetings you didn't need to attend, or menial tasks that didn't matter. Deliberately eliminate these things from your schedule as you move forward.

Next, determine what to automate. These are repetitive activities that you can automate electronically or create a system that reduces the time required to do them. For example, if you frequently receive emails that make similar types of requests, create an email template that you can copy and paste. This saves you the time of writing the same email from scratch again and again. Other examples of automation include data collection, automated bill payment, creating workflows, or using a platform to schedule social media posts.

Finally, delegate tasks that must be done (but not by you). Again, your goal is to stay focused on your highest priorities. Therefore, delegate as much as possible to an administrative assistant, another team member, an intern, or a volunteer. You might even outsource a task to an outside vendor.

- **Couple Energy Rhythms with Batching**—We all have times of the day when we function at our very best. Figure out the ebb and flow of your energy rhythms, and then allocate responsibilities accordingly. In addition, batch similar activities together. For example, consider batching administrative tasks, receipts, and communication in one block of time (one that has a lower energy rhythm). Or use one large chunk of time to accomplish a single task that requires a high level of creativity.

I use the mornings to write, prepare sermons, and work on projects that require my best thinking. I batch these tasks in the morning because that's when my energy rhythm is the strongest. I also batch my one-on-one meetings with our staff on Monday afternoons. These meetings occur during a single afternoon, one right after another, rather than spacing them throughout the week. When you know your energy rhythms and batch your time accordingly, you'll get more done in less time.

There are plenty of ideas for working more efficiently, but these five practices will give you a massive head start. The second part of the "How" circle is boundaries.

Boundaries are the guardrails that protect the use of your time. Without boundaries, somebody else will determine how you spend your time. Here are five tips to help you establish clear boundaries with your schedule.

- **Conduct a Time Audit**—A seven-day time audit will help you discover how you're spending your time at work, home, and everywhere in between. Plus, a time audit will clarify where you need to establish stronger boundaries. Without this knowledge, your boundaries may be incomplete or insufficient.
- **Address the Root Cause of an Out-of-Control Schedule**—Two big drivers of an out-of-control schedule are fear and approval. For example, many people work long hours because they're afraid they'll let the boss down or, worse, lose their job. When it comes to approval, some people overwork

because it's how they receive affirmation from others. They become addicted to approval and, therefore, allocate disproportionate amounts of time to certain areas and activities. To create healthy boundaries, you must address the root cause of your behavior. How is fear and the need for approval driving the use of your time?

- **Create a Yes/No Framework**—You will have dozens of requests come across your desk every week. Determine ahead of time what you will say yes to and what you will say no to. Once you establish your yes/no framework, communicate these boundaries to your family, assistant, and other leaders in your inner circle.
- **Establish Meeting Time Blocks**—Meetings often go long, and people will assume you have nothing else to do if you haven't established a clear boundary. Therefore, identify and communicate when you will do meetings and how much time you have available to meet. One way to do this is to schedule meetings back-to-back. This creates a built-in boundary that requires the meeting to end in time for the next one to start. For example, when scheduling an appointment, say, "I can meet you at 3:00 p.m. I have another meeting that will start at 3:30, but you'll have my undivided attention during our time together."
- **Implement Technology Boundaries**—Technology is a wonderful gift—until it's not. While technology can help us be incredibly efficient, it can also make us endlessly distracted. Case in point: the average person spends 143 minutes per day on social media.[54] That represents 15 percent of our waking hours. Imagine what you could do if you

put half of that time back into your annual calendar. That would equal 435 hours. That's the equivalent of fifty-four eight-hour workdays every year. Set boundaries to keep technology from becoming your biggest time thief.

I like to refer to the strategies for *planning* and *boundaries* as my 5 x 5. The five planning practices combined with the five boundary strategies create a multiplying effect on my time. Again, there are plenty of tips and tricks to time management, but this 5 x 5 approach will give you a great start.

LIVE IN THE SWEET SPOT

The sweet spot of time management is where the three circles overlap. When the WHY, WHERE, and HOW of time management intersect, you're able to allocate the precious minutes of your life to:

- Fulfill your life purpose
- Live out your values
- Serve in roles aligned with your purpose
- Invest time in priorities that matter most
- Make each minute count
- Live in the boundaries that keep you healthy

This can only happen when you clarify your WHY (purpose and values), identify your WHERE (roles and priorities), and establish your HOW (planning and boundaries). What happens when one of these time management keys is missing?

- Time management without purpose and values equals an UNFULFILLED LIFE.
- Time management without roles and priorities equals an UNFOCUSED LIFE.

- Time management without planning and boundaries equals an UNHEALTHY LIFE.

To make your greatest impact, your time management strategy needs all three circles and the six keys within them. This is how you get insanely practical about time management. Check out Leadership Tool #5: The 3 Circles Time Tool to help you get started. The sweet spot of time management is where you'll experience the greatest fulfillment, focus, and health.

INSANELY PRACTICAL REFLECTION AND DISCUSSION

1. What's the "bigger yes" burning inside of you that should receive a larger allocation of your time?
2. Have you ever considered the role purpose and values (Circle #1) play in time management? What needs to be your first step to gain greater clarity in this area?
3. What roles and priorities (Circle #2) are best aligned with your current understanding of your purpose and values? How can you allocate more time to them?
4. Which two tips for time management would help you better maximize Circle #3 (Planning and Boundaries)?

LEADERSHIP TOOL #5
The 3 Circles Time Tool

Insanely practical time management happens at the intersection of three circles: WHY (Purpose and Values), WHERE (Roles and Priorities), and HOW (Planning and Boundaries). Use the chart below to create a master plan for your time that defines each circle.

NAME:				
WHY: PURPOSE and VALUES	MY LIFE PURPOSE:			
	MY CORE VALUES:			
WHERE: ROLES and PRIORITIES	ROLE #1:			
	3 PRIORITIES:			
	ROLE #2:			
	3 PRIORITIES:			
	ROLE #3:			
	3 PRIORITIES:			
	ROLE #4:			
	3 PRIORITIES:			
	ROLE #5:			
	3 PRIORITIES:			

HOW: PLANNING and BOUNDARIES	TIME MANAGEMENT TOOL				
	WEEKLY MEETING DAY/TIME				
	MY BIG 3 (DAY/WEEK)	WHAT I'LL ELIMINATE	WHAT I'LL AUTOMATE	WHAT I'LL DELEGATE	WHAT I'LL BATCH
	MY PRIMARY BOUNDARIES				

Download The 3 Circles Time Tool at insanelypracticalleadership.com.

CHAPTER 6

HOW TO MAKE LEADERSHIP DECISIONS

"Whenever you see a successful business, someone once made a courageous decision."
—Peter F. Drucker

On September 16, 2012, Karen, I, and a fantastic group of committed volunteers planted 7 City Church in the heart of the twelfth largest city in the United States—Fort Worth, Texas.[55] We're located in the cultural arts and West 7th area, right outside of downtown. It's a busy and bustling part of the city, and the church is surrounded by apartments, lofts, restaurants, retail space, and as I mentioned earlier, twenty bars filled with large crowds of inebriated partiers. Let's just say, weekends are wild.

What I didn't tell you about this area is that property is expensive, and parking comes at a premium. Our building is landlocked between a busy intersection on one corner and a four-story apartment complex on the other corner. We don't own a single parking space. Instead, we rent parking from a large, historic football stadium across the street that's owned by Fort Worth's school district.

After people park on Sunday mornings, they stand patiently at a crosswalk as traffic zooms by. When the flashing crosswalk light indicates it's safe to proceed, congregants cross a four-lane street and then walk to the front door. Sometimes, it feels like a replay of the classic video game *Frogger*, but thankfully, our parking team does a great job helping people safely cross the street. That's the reality of church planting in the city.

Several years ago, our building reached a tipping point. Our auditorium was full, and our kid's space stretched thin. I still remember a family walking into the auditorium one Sunday morning while I was on the stage speaking. They stood at the back, looking for a place to sit. I silently cringed inside, realizing this family was visiting for the first time. I thought to myself, *We have to do* something *to alleviate the pressure and make room for more people*. In the weeks that followed, I realized we had two options: renovate or relocate.

The first option was to renovate our existing space. By reworking our floorplan, we could incorporate some unused space into our auditorium and kid's environments. But this solution also had its challenges. If we tipped over the "renovation domino," we'd have to bring a very old building up to city code. Renovation would require an electrical overhaul, new plumbing, seven new HVAC systems, asbestos abatement, and the installation of a fire sprinkler system—and that's before you make anything look pretty. Just fixing the bones of the building would wield a hefty price tag.

The second option was to relocate. However, because we have a vision for the heart of the city, relocating to a larger building *with* adequate parking would be like searching for a needle in a haystack. There just aren't that many options near downtown. On top of that, moving would be painfully long and exorbitant in cost.

In short, we had two options: *expensive* or *more expensive*.

A decision loomed before us: do we renovate or relocate? Do we launch a major construction project or search for land? Do we remain landlocked in our existing space or look for a bigger building? Those aren't the options pastors hope for, but that was our reality.

NAVIGATING THE DECISION

Recognizing the enormity and complexity of this decision, I was reminded of James's words: "If you need wisdom, ask our generous God, and he will give it to you. He will not rebuke you for asking" (James 1:5). I certainly needed wisdom, and I didn't want to make a giant decision without the Holy Spirit's direction. So, I took James's advice and began to pray.

"God, what should we do?"

"Should we renovate or relocate?"

"Lord, fill me with the wisdom and knowledge of Your perfect will."

Prayer by prayer. God began to guide us and lead us.

In addition to praying, I began researching our attendance trends to better understand our specific needs. I assessed overcrowded rooms, sketched out floorplans, and imagined future possibilities. But I also knew this decision was far bigger than me. So, one night, I presented the challenges to our board. I shared my research, the pain points we were experiencing, and our need for more space. The board was very receptive, and over the coming months, we weighed our options and considered the best path forward.

After lengthy discussions and careful deliberation, we finally decided to redesign and renovate our existing space. By utilizing the unused part of our facility, we could increase the size of our auditorium by 50 percent and enlarge our kid's ministry space to match it. However, because our building was over eighty years old, we also needed the expert advice of an architect.

In the coming weeks, we hired an architectural firm to look at our building, determine its structural soundness, identify our limiting factors, and present us with several designs. The last thing I wanted to do was tip over a wall that tipped over the whole building, which we later discovered was a real possibility. When we suggested expanding the depth of the auditorium by moving the back wall, the architect said, "That's a shear wall. If you knock it down, you're at risk of the front and back walls of the building falling over." Note to self: don't move that wall.

CURVE BALL

I'll never forget the day when we received the design with the estimated cost of construction. As I reviewed the plans, I took a giant gulp, recognizing we didn't have the money to build what the architect proposed. I presented it to the board, and we quickly realized our need to launch a major vision campaign to raise the money. However, funding of this magnitude was new territory for us, so we decided to hire a consultant to help us get started. Over the next six months, the consultant helped us craft a generosity campaign, and in September of that year, we launched a two-year vision to raise several million dollars.

After receiving financial pledges from the congregation for the campaign, we began searching for a general contractor. I'd heard horror stories of "pastor becomes contractor," and I knew my story would be no better without professional help. Therefore, we interviewed three contractors and had them present proposals to our board. We were careful to review the details in each proposal, ask hard questions, and then pick the contractor right for the job.

In the weeks that followed, the general contractor reviewed the architectural designs to establish a cost estimate. To our surprise, the price increased by more than 20 percent from what the architect had originally estimated. I still remember sitting in a meeting when a board member said, "Stephen, we can't build this design. Our monthly mortgage payment would be way beyond what we can afford." I knew they were right, but I also knew we desperately needed the space.

Weighing our options, we agreed to request additional, less expensive designs. I met with our architect and said, "I need you to shave a million dollars off this project. I don't know how you can do it, but our auditorium and kid's space are our highest priority." The architect began slicing and dicing, looking for cost savings while maintaining our vision for excellence. They came back with a manageable plan that looked great, and that revised design became our pathway forward.

Later that year, we were ready to begin construction—with one condition. I told our contractor that because space is so prime near downtown, they had to keep us in the building *during* construction. That decision lengthened the timeline by three months, but the only other option was to move off-campus, rent space in a high-dollar district, secure the equipment for a portable set-up, and risk losing momentum.

Thankfully, the general contractor came up with a workable plan to unfold the construction in stages. Then, every Monday, crews arrived bright and early, and every Friday at noon, the work stopped so a team could clean the building. We had services on Sunday morning, and then the process repeated itself week after week for the next nine months.

Was it worth it? Was all the planning, the hassle, the meetings, and the countless decisions worth the blood, sweat, and tears? Absolutely! The big day finally arrived when we celebrated our grand opening. An eighty-year-old building had been transformed inside, and after lots of praying, planning, and sacrifice, we gave thanks to God for His faithful provision. Most importantly, we had the space to reach, equip, and serve more people. One giant leadership decision—which led to countless smaller decisions—turned into a beautiful celebration.

HOW TO MAKE LEADERSHIP DECISIONS

Making leadership decisions is hard, and when the decisions stack up like bricks on a building or papers on a messy desk, it's easy to feel overwhelmed by decision fatigue. Choosing to renovate our building was the *big* decision, but it unlocked a multitude of smaller decisions about designs, contractors, finishes, features to keep, ideas to cut, and how to cast vision and raise funds.

That brings up an important question: how do you make good leadership decisions? How do you choose the right path, ensuring it won't backfire when you desperately need the support of others to see it through to completion? Good decision-making requires ten core ingredients, each coupled with an important question.[56]

> **Lacking wisdom isn't a sin; it's simply the condition we often find ourselves in.**

1) PRAYER: Have I asked for the Holy Spirit's wisdom?

As I contemplated the alternatives to secure adequate space, my first step was to ask God for wisdom. Praying and pondering became inseparable as we determined how to remain faithful to our vision for the center of the city. Proverbs 1:7 says, "Start with GOD—the first step in learning is bowing down to GOD; only fools thumb their noses at such wisdom and learning" (MSG). Don't despise the wisdom that is freely available to you. Ask God. His wisdom is infinite because He is omniscient.

Lacking wisdom isn't a sin; it's simply the condition we often find ourselves in. But again, James gives us a clear directive when those conditions arise: "If you need wisdom, ask our generous God" (James 1:5). And this isn't a one-time request either. Jesus said to keep on asking, keep on seeking, and keep on knocking (Matthew 7:7). He even told His disciples that they should always pray and never give up (Luke 18:1). Prayer—combined with the truth of God's Word—is a powerful source of wisdom.

Some would argue that prayer is the only decision-making key that matters. However, in my experience, God often uses the other keys to confirm His voice, deepen our understanding, and create buy-in from other leaders.

2) DNA: Does the decision support our organizational identity?

Every organization has a unique DNA that consists of four factors: beliefs, vision, mission, and values. *Beliefs* are the foundation of the organization. For 7 City Church, our beliefs are the inspired truths of our faith. They anchor the church and provide a strong footing on which to build. *Vision* is the preferred future you feel called to pursue. It's the better tomorrow that you see in your mind's eye today. *Mission* describes why the organization exists and what it does. When you do your mission, it should lead to the fulfillment of your vision. Finally, *values* are the guiding principles and priorities that influence how you behave and where you invest time, energy, and money.

When you make decisions, be true to the organization's DNA. If your decisions violate your DNA, it's only a matter of time before you wake up to a future you never intended to create. Our decision to renovate our building didn't oppose our organizational DNA. Quite the opposite; it facilitated our ability to fulfill our vision in a greater measure.

3) RESEARCH: Have I done my homework?

Big decisions minus deep research equals agonizing regret. Jesus gave this warning:

> *"Suppose one of you wants to build a tower. Won't you first sit down and estimate the cost to see if you have enough*

money to complete it? For if you lay the foundation and are not able to finish it, everyone who sees it will ridicule you, saying, 'This person began to build and wasn't able to finish.'" —Luke 14:28-30 (NIV)

Research helps you clarify the real issues at hand. I didn't want us to design a building that looked cool but was functionally irrelevant. That's why our architect started by researching our attendance patterns and capacity issues. We had to understand our restraints before we could develop a path forward. In addition, research helps you quantify the time, energy, and money needed to turn the decision into reality. There's always a price tag, and research helps you define it. Whatever you do, steer clear of the extremes. Don't get trapped in paralysis by analysis and avoid becoming the victim of impulsive regret. Your job as a leader is not to have all the answers, but to create a space that facilitates research and innovation so the answers can emerge.

4) EXPERIENCE: Do lessons from past experience support the decision?

Past lessons should inform future decisions. I encourage leaders to consider two types of experience: *personal experience* and *organizational experience*. Personal experience helps you glean wisdom from your own failures, successes, habits, education, and observations. Organizational experience draws on the organization's history, trends, metrics, wins, and setbacks. If you do a good job *mining* this pool of experience, you'll discover important lessons to help you make better decisions.

One thing to keep in mind is that experience *informs* your decisions; it doesn't *dictate* your decisions. Learn from the past while leaning into the future. And when your experience is shallow, take the next step—seek advice.

5) ADVICE: Does the wisdom of others affirm the decision?

As we pondered and prepared for the building renovation, we sought outside advice. I spoke to pastors with experience in building projects. I talked regularly with a close friend who works with a church construction company. We secured a consultant to help us raise significant amounts of money. We hired an architect and a contractor to create designs and do the construction. I can't imagine how many mistakes we would have made without these outside voices.

Seeking advice is especially important when you're making complex decisions or legal decisions. It's also critical in judgments where you have little expertise or are facing a significant barrier to progress. In these situations, be an aggressive learner who seeks outside perspectives from coaches, consultants, and wise leaders.

> **The last time I checked, God can do immeasurably more than you can think, ask, or imagine. Stop putting handcuffs on God.**

I recently met with a high-capacity leader for sixty minutes. I didn't know if I'd ever get this opportunity again, so I spent seven hours preparing for the meeting. I listened to a couple of interviews of this leader, scripted thoughtful questions, organized my questions by category, and then put them in the order of importance. When my preparation was complete, I had thirty-three questions, knowing I'd be lucky to ask ten of them before time ran out. But I'd rather run out of time than run out of questions. When the day to meet finally came, I only made it through seven questions. But seven hours of preparation for the answers to seven timely questions was worth every minute. I maximized the moment so I could maximize my growth. That's the approach to take when you're seeking advice from wise leaders. Be prepared.

6) RESOURCES: Can we get the money to start and sustain the decision?

Money doesn't grow on trees, but I have other news for you: money doesn't follow fear either. Instead of saying, "We don't have the money," start asking, "Can we get the money to start and sustain the decision?" Notice that this question addresses two important resource realities.

First, it asks, "Can we get the money?" The last time I checked, God can do immeasurably more than you can think, ask, or imagine (Ephesians 3:20). Stop putting handcuffs on God. Just because you don't *have* the money doesn't mean you can't *get* the money. We didn't have the cash to renovate, so we launched a vision campaign to secure the money for the project.

Second, the resource question focuses on starting *and* sustaining the decision. We needed cash to not only begin construction but also make monthly payments on the money we borrowed. That's why we went back to our architect and asked him to shave a million dollars off the project. We weren't going to jeopardize the financial stability of the church to construct a project with an unsustainable monthly payment.

The resource question is a bit of a mindbender. It requires *faith* to look beyond your current resources and *wisdom* to chart a sustainable path forward. Without faith, you'll say no to every opportunity that doesn't fit neatly in the confines of your current account balance. And without wisdom, you'll overextend yourself and handicap your future.

7) IMPACT: Will the decision deliver a good return on investment?

Doing research, reflecting on experience, acquiring advice, and answering the resource question will help you determine the decision's impact. However, you also want to ask four questions to help you evaluate the upside and downside of the decision:

- *What do we stand to gain by making this decision?*
- *What do we risk losing by making this decision?*
- *What do we risk losing by NOT making this decision?*
- *Is the return on investment worth the risk?*

Every decision creates impact. Your job is to determine if the return on investment is worth it. When we decided to renovate our building, we knew it would be costly. And when we launched a vision campaign, we knew we'd likely lose some members. Both were true, but the return on investment was worth the risk.

8) INTUITION: Is my gut telling me to proceed?

Intuition is the most nuanced part of decision-making. After all, how can a hunch inform your decisions? Intuition plays out in two ways.

First, intuition stems from giftedness. John Maxwell observed that we are most intuitive in the areas of our greatest giftedness.[57] For example, if you're a gifted musician, you'll be intuitive in your preferred instrument. If you're a gifted communicator, you'll be intuitive about connecting with your audience. If you're a gifted business leader, you'll be intuitive in running a strong business. To help you make good decisions, pay attention to your gift-informed intuition.

Second, intuition comes from the Holy Spirit. The Holy Spirit is the Spirit of Truth (John 16:33), and He never leads us astray. The early church understood these Spirit-led nudges and once even concluded, "It seemed good to the Holy Spirit and to us" (Acts 15:28). Their Spirit-informed perception helped them make good decisions.

9) INFLUENCE: Are my key leaders receptive and supportive?

There's an old proverb that says, "If you want to go fast, go alone. If you want to go far, go together." In leadership, *going together* means making sure your influencers—staff, board, and key leaders—are *with you* in the decision. You can have the greatest ideas in the world—even ideas inspired by God—and yet fail to move forward because your leaders aren't on board. There are three ways to ensure your leaders are receptive and supportive.

First, include your leaders in the decision-making process. Deliberately seek their perspective. As the old saying goes, "People are down on what they're not up on." The most important posture you can take with your leaders is to *stop selling* and *start listening*. If you sell your solutions before listening to their perspective, you'll never garner the support you need from the people who can help you the most. Calm your insecurities, seek their perspective, and welcome it with gratitude.

Second, *test* a direction without *declaring* a decision. Too often, leaders declare a decision publicly without first testing the waters privately. Bounce your idea off a few trusted people who will be most affected by your decision. Say, "I've been thinking about . . ." or "What would be your thoughts if we tried something like . . . ?" When you test a direction before declaring a decision, you create space for people to warm up to your ideas.

Third, communicate the decision in layers. Once a decision is made, communicate it throughout the layers of influence within the organization. Think about these layers as concentric circles representing your staff, board, key leaders, and volunteers. Start with your inner circle, and then move outward until the decision has been communicated throughout the entire organization. This strategy creates buy-in with your most influential leaders, and it helps you discover objections and concerns. When pushback arises, you'll have time to adjust your vision-casting talk to address these objections before you communicate to the next layer of the organization.

I garnered support from key influencers by first speaking to our staff and board. Then, when the time came to cast the vision to a broader audience, we shared it with our financial partners and volunteers. By the time we cast the vision publicly on a Sunday morning, half of the congregation had already heard it. This communication strategy gave time for influencers to absorb the decision, get their questions answered, and buy into the vision.

10) TIMING: Is the timing right for the leader, team, and organization?

The right decision at the wrong time is a lost opportunity. When the timing is right, buy-in increases. When the timing is right, your credibility as a leader goes up. And when the timing is right, the impact on the organization multiplies. Timing is not one-dimensional, which is why decisions require you to weigh timing from three perspectives.

First, is the timing right for the *leader*? Leaders feel the brunt of the biggest decisions, and they always take an emotional, mental, physical, relational, and financial toll. If your reserves aren't adequate when you make the decision, you'll pay a heavy price.

Second, is the timing right for the *team*? The bigger the decision, the more energy it will take to implement it. When we launched our vision, it required all hands on deck to see the very best results. If your team doesn't have the time, energy, or buy-in to get the decision off the ground, it's not the right time.

Third, is the timing right for the *organization*? Change is difficult for organizations, especially if you're dealing with a lot of tradition. If people aren't prepared to embrace the ramifications of a big decision, then your implementation may be premature. Have a few more meetings with key leaders and develop a slightly longer runway to get airborne.

> **Conditions are rarely perfect to make a big decision.**

We didn't launch our vision campaign until the timing was right for all three—the leaders, the team, and the organization. First, the *leaders* took the time to secure a solid plan from the architect and consultant. Second, the *team* had the necessary runway to implement the vision campaign. And third, we launched the vision at a time in the year that was optimal for the greatest participation from the *church*.

One word of caution about timing. Conditions are rarely *perfect* to make a big decision. Therefore, don't delay a decision indefinitely. Be wise about the timing while courageously committing to act.

CHECK YOUR DASHBOARD

Imagine the ten decision-making questions as lights on a dashboard. Each light is green, yellow, or red. When you can give an emphatic "Yes" to each decision-making question, the light turns green. If your answer is mixed or incomplete, the light turns yellow. And if your answer is a clear "No," then the light turns red. When you're making decisions, you want as many lights as possible to turn green.

If too many lights are red, making the decision will produce negative results. Think about it like this:

- Without *Prayer*, decisions lack supernatural wisdom.

- Without *DNA*, decisions lack organizational alignment.
- Without *Research*, decisions lack depth.
- Without *Experience*, decisions lack maturity.
- Without *Advice*, decisions lack perspective.
- Without *Resources*, decisions lack progress.
- Without *Impact*, decisions lack return on investment.
- Without *Intuition*, decisions lack peace.
- Without *Influencers*, decisions lack buy-in.
- Without *Timing*, decisions lack success.

Each ingredient plays an important role, and together, they help you make wise decisions that deliver great outcomes.

THE FAITH FACTOR

While you want as many lights as possible to turn green on your Decision-Making Dashboard, the process also involves faith. We counted the cost of our building renovation, but after doing our homework and answering each question, an element of risk remained. We didn't know what surprises were lurking behind the walls of an old building. We didn't know how much money would actually be donated during the campaign. We didn't know what delays the project would encounter.

That's the nature of big decisions. There will always be an element of risk cloaked in unknowns and what-ifs. But if you're waiting for 100 percent assurance of success, you'll never make a decision. You must lead in the face of uncertainty by securing the facts and then taking informed steps of faith. Faith doesn't replace the ten questions, but it's an essential companion in the process.

To help you put this decision-making framework into practice, utilize Leadership Tool #6: The Decision-Making Dashboard. As you do, not only will you make better decisions, but you'll experience greater buy-in from the people you lead.

INSANELY PRACTICAL REFLECTION AND DISCUSSION

1. When was a time you made a leadership decision that didn't turn out well? After reading this chapter, what would you do differently?
2. What part of the decision-making framework is your biggest weakness? How could you shore up that weakness to make better and wiser decisions in the future?
3. What role has faith played in your decision-making? How do you balance faith with the Decision-Making Dashboard?
4. What decision do you need to make soon, and how will you leverage the Decision-Making Dashboard in the process?

LEADERSHIP TOOL #6
Decision-Making Dashboard

Use the Decision-Making Dashboard below to help you make good decisions. First, in twenty words or less, describe a decision you need to make. Then, answer each decision-making question. In addition, give a rating (Green, Yellow, or Red) to each question. Green means you have a clear "Yes" to the question. Yellow means you have mixed support for the question. Red means your answer is predominantly "No." Based on your responses and ratings, articulate your decision at the bottom of the dashboard.

DECISION-MAKING DASHBOARD			
DECISION DESCRIPTION (In less than 20 words)			
Decision-Making Questions & Responses	Overall Rating		
	Green	Yellow	Red
PRAYER: Have I asked for the Holy Spirit's Wisdom?			
DNA: Does the decision support our organizational identity?			
RESEARCH: Have I done my homework?			
EXPERIENCE: Do lessons from past experience support the decision?			
ADVICE: Does the wisdom of others affirm the decision?			

RESOURCES: Can we get the money to start and sustain the decision?
IMPACT: Will the decision deliver a good return on investment?
INTUITION: Is my gut telling me to proceed?
INFLUENCE: Are my key leaders receptive and supportive?
TIMING: Is the timing right for the leader, team, and organization?
Based on my responses above, the Green/Yellow/Red ratings, and the faith factor, what decision should I make or what steps should I take?

Download the Decision-Making Dashboard at insanelypracticalleadership.com.

PART 2
MASTER THE ART OF LEADING OTHERS

CHAPTER 7
HOW TO BUILD INFLUENCE

"Anytime you influence the thinking, beliefs, or development of another person, you're engaging in leadership."
—**Ken Blanchard and Mark Miller**

Each year, *TIME* publishes its list of the one hundred most influential people. The list includes artists, icons, pioneers, leaders, titans, and innovators. Over the years, *TIME* has featured a wide variety of people, such as Apple titan Tim Cook, and actor, producer, and trailblazer Tyler Perry. Other list-makers are lesser-known but are still making a significant contribution, like Catherine Coleman Flowers who is fighting for justice in places like Lowndes County, Alabama, where 40 percent of the majority-Black residents lack access to clean sanitation.[58]

Athletes, actors, and political leaders are highlighted, as well as business tycoons and social entrepreneurs. Interestingly, some people are here today and gone tomorrow. And I must admit, I've never even heard of some of these influencers.

What about you? If you assembled a list of the most influential people in history, who would make your top one hundred? I'd no doubt recognize some of the names, while others would be obscure to the world but deeply impactful to you. Our top one hundred would vary greatly, but one person on my list would be the apostle Paul.

MEET PAUL

Outside of Jesus, arguably the most influential person in the New Testament was the apostle Paul. At birth, Paul's Jewish name was Saul, and as a member of the Jewish tribe of Benjamin, he was likely named after the famed first king of Israel.[59] But, because he was a Roman citizen, Saul's Latin name was *Paullus* (or "Paul" in the Greek).[60] As Acts 13:9 notes, Saul was also known as Paul, and throughout this chapter, I'll use both names interchangeably.

Paul's influence was broad and profound. He conducted at least three missionary journeys, bringing the gospel to the Gentiles, kings, and Jews in places like Galatia, Macedonia, Achaia, and Asia (Acts 9:15). German Theologian and New Testament professor Eckhard J. Schnabel estimates Paul traveled some 15,500 miles during his ministry, and 8,700 of those miles were by foot.[61] Throughout his travels, Paul not only preached the gospel, performed miracles, and equipped leaders, but he also suffered countless hardships in the process.

Paul's influence was compounded by the churches he started in cities and regions like Philippi, Galatia, Ephesus, Cyprus, and Crete. While many scholars attribute fourteen churches to Paul, author Neil Cole observes, "He probably started close to 20 churches himself, with many more born out of those by his apprentice leaders."[62]

In addition to his preaching and church planting, Paul wrote nearly a third of the New Testament. His Spirit-inspired letters to Timothy, Titus, the Philippians, the Corinthians, and others are his most significant contributions to the Christian faith. Since his death, dozens of books have been written about Paul, and millions of sermons have been preached from the letters he wrote. Without question, Paul's influence is substantial and significant.

But that's not where his story began.

Saul was once a fierce and unflinching opponent of Christianity. When a follower of Jesus named Stephen was falsely accused of blasphemy, Saul watched in agreement as Stephen was stoned to death (Acts 7:58; 8:1). Then, a huge wave of persecution swept over the church in Jerusalem as Saul dragged men and women out of their homes, threw them in prison, and embarked on a mission to destroy the church (Acts 8:2-3). Saul's zeal fueled his influence as he relentlessly persecuted followers of the Way. He was "hounding some to death," (Acts 22:4), and he admitted, "I was so violently opposed to them that I even chased them down in foreign cities" (Acts 26:11).

Saul's harassment, oppression, and torture were unyielding. When speaking of the believers in Jerusalem, he said, "I cast my vote against them when they were condemned to death" (Acts 26:10). In a fervent, unrestrained passion for his religious beliefs and traditions, Saul threatened arrest, forced imprisonment, and killed Christians to purge the world of Jesus's influence.

HOW TO BUILD INFLUENCE

Paul's story raises an important question: how did a man who nodded his approval to the death of Christ-followers become an avid proponent of Jesus? How did a zealous Pharisee who tyrannized Christians become the most influential leader in the early church? Paul's post-persecution influence was shaped by five ingredients, and those qualities are the foundation for building God-honoring influence today.

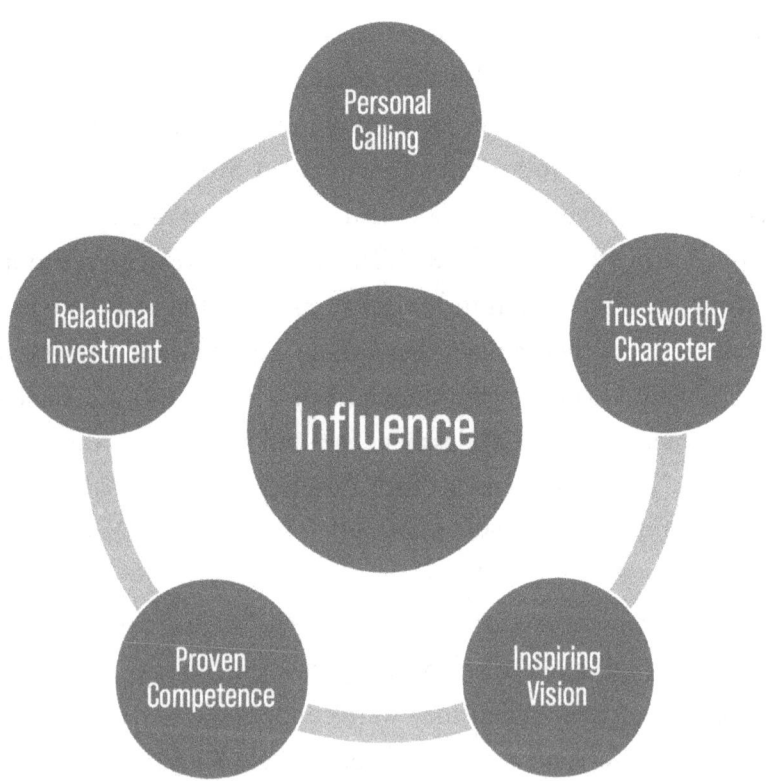

1) Personal Calling

Saul went from an ardent persecutor to a passionate preacher of the gospel after one pivotal moment: a transformational encounter with Jesus. As he traveled to Damascus, eager to kill the Lord's followers, "A light from heaven suddenly shone down around him. He fell to the ground and heard a voice saying to him, 'Saul! Saul! Why are you persecuting me?'" (Acts 9:3-4) Unsure of who was speaking to him, Saul said, "Who are you, lord?" . . . the voice replied, "I am Jesus, the one you are persecuting! Now get up and go into the city, and you will be told what you must do" (Acts 9:5-6).

During this crucial moment, Saul was struck blind for three days until a believer named Ananias prayed for him. Initially, Ananias objected to the idea, reminding the Lord of Saul's reputation for persecuting Christians. But the Lord said, "Go, for Saul is my chosen instrument to take my message to the Gentiles and to kings, as well as to the people of Israel. And I will show him how much he must suffer for my name's sake" (Acts 9:15-16).

Ananias obeyed the Lord, Saul's eyes were opened, and he was filled with the Holy Spirit. The man who once persecuted followers of Jesus was now a follower himself. But after a season of preaching in Damascus and Jerusalem, he faced his own threat of death, returned home to Tarsus, and for the next decade—roughly 36 to 46 AD—Saul was benched (see Acts 9:28-30).

But why?

Why would Saul have a radical encounter with Jesus, burst into a flurry of ministry, and then be sidelined for a decade? It turns out, Saul's decade of silence prepared him for his divine calling.

Author and theologian N.T. Wright observed, "Saul spent a silent decade deepening the well of scriptural reflection from which he would thereafter draw the water he needed."[63] This reflection helped him reconcile his life-altering Jesus encounter with the Scriptures. In addition, Paul experienced personal revelation from Jesus Himself. In his letter to the Galatians, he said:

> *Dear brothers and sisters, I want you to understand that the gospel message I preach is not based on mere human reasoning. I received my message from no human source, and no one taught me. Instead, I received it by direct revelation from Jesus Christ.* —Galatians 1:11-12

Furthermore, Paul used this time to probe the culture of Tarsus, expanding his knowledge of the Gentile world he was called to reach. Author Neil Cole observed, "Tarsus was a good place to be stationed if you were to learn how to evangelize the Gentiles, for it was a renowned cultural center for teaching philosophy, rhetoric, and law."[64]

Notice three distinct aspects of Saul's calling.

First, *Saul was called to a Person*. His calling was grounded in a personal encounter with Jesus on the road to Damascus, which catalyzed a lifelong pursuit of Him.

Second, *Saul was called to preach*. God told Ananias that He had chosen Saul to take the gospel to Gentiles, kings, and Jews. These first two aspects of Saul's calling are captured in Galatians 1: "But even before I was born, God chose me and called me by his marvelous grace. Then, it pleased him to reveal his Son to me" (vv. 15-16). Notice, Saul was first called to the Person of Jesus. Then, he continues, "... so that I would proclaim the Good News about Jesus to the Gentiles" (v. 16). After calling him to Himself, the Lord called Saul to preach the gospel to specific groups of people.

Third, *Saul was prepared for his calling*. For ten years, Saul mined the Scriptures, encountered revelations from Jesus, and carefully dissected the culture he was called to reach. Saul's silent decade became a catalyst for his calling.

You, too, are called.

> **Your calling is the internal driver that defines the external arena where your influence will come to life.**

First, like Saul, Jesus calls you to follow Him. Only in Christ will you find the hope, forgiveness, and redemption your heart longs to experience. Second, from your relationship with Jesus will come a calling to serve and lead. This calling (as I noted in chapter 5), will flow out of your God-given gifts, knowledge, and passions. Third, God will prepare you for His calling through a unique blend of spiritual formation, personal experiences, and tests and trials.

That raises an important question: what on earth does calling have to do with influence? In the same way a laser amplifies light to cut through metal, your calling amplifies your influence to make its greatest impact. Your calling—those unique good works God created you to do (Ephesians 2:10)—focuses your time, energy, and resources on what matters most. Your calling is the internal driver that defines the external arena where your influence will come to life.

If you're called to create beautiful paintings, the arena of art is where your influence will flourish. If you're called to raise kids who love Jesus, your family will be the arena where your calling is fulfilled. If you're called to lead at an executive level, the business world is the arena where your influence will blossom. When your calling is clear, your influence will grow in a specific arena of culture, whether it's business, education, government, healthcare, arts, entertainment, media, the church, the social sector, or your family. Your calling reveals where you're most likely to have influence.

2) Trustworthy Character

Author Kevin Myers describes character as the *first base* in life and leadership. He illustrates the importance of character by posing a simple question: "Who draws the lines in your life?" The lines represent our character, and as Myers observes, "Whoever controls the 'pencil' in your life draws the lines."[65] For some people, their character lines are drawn by family, friends, educators, the media, political parties, or even their own feelings. But to become an effective leader, you must put the pencil in God's hands and let Him draw the lines of right and wrong so He can build His character within you.

That's what Paul did. He put the pencil in God's hands, and as a result, he developed a trustworthy character that others could confidently follow. In fact, Paul told the Corinthian church, "Follow my example, as I follow the example of Christ" (1 Corinthians 11:1, NIV). He gave the same instructions to the church in Philippi: "Dear brothers and sisters, pattern your lives after mine, and learn from those who follow our example" (Philippians 3:17). And to the Ephesian elders, he said, "And I have been a constant example of how you can help those in need by working hard" (Acts 20:35).

Paul didn't stop with his own example. He also implored Timothy to set an example worth following: "Don't let anyone think less of you because you are young. Be an example to all believers in what you say, in the way you live, in your love, your faith, and your purity" (1 Timothy 4:12). And he told Titus,

"In the same way, encourage the young men to live wisely. And you yourself must be an example to them by doing good works of every kind. Let everything you do reflect the integrity and seriousness of your teaching" (Titus 2:6-7). Each of these passages reveals how Paul's example of trustworthy character powered his influence.

Without consistent integrity, your influence is fleeting—like a viral video that produces fifteen minutes of fame before fading into oblivion. But when your character is trustworthy, it impacts the width, depth, and weight of your influence.

First, trustworthy character enlarges the *width* of your influence. Character enables you to influence more people because it gives them a reason to trust you. Without character, influence leaks. The holes in your character are the drains of your influence.

> **Without trustworthy character, you'll kick the legs out from under your influence. But with trustworthy character, you'll stand under the weight of leadership without it crushing you.**

Next, trustworthy character increases the *depth* of your influence. The more trustworthy you are, the more people will allow you to influence them at the deepest levels. Deep trust exists when character has been tested by hardship. When people see you make wise decisions, treat people with dignity, and maintain your integrity—all while the storms of adversity are raging—they'll trust you. That's when your character speaks the loudest, and your influence grows the strongest. Truth be told, you can't develop deep character roots without the storms of life. As author and pastor Mark Batterson observed, "What makes us think we can be conformed to the image of Christ without being betrayed by Judas, criticized by Pharisees, or tempted by the devil himself?"[66] That's where true character is forged.

Finally, trustworthy character supports the *weight* of your influence. Leadership becomes heavier and harder as your responsibilities become bigger and broader. Without trustworthy character, you'll kick the legs out from under your influence. But with trustworthy character, you'll stand under the weight of leadership without it crushing you.

Untrustworthy leaders exert a great deal of energy to conceal their secrets and cover their sins. They live in a constant state of deal-making and rule-bending. But leaders with solid character live with a sense of security because the foundation of their lives is built on truth. They don't have anything to prove or anything to hide. Solomon said, "Whoever walks in integrity walks securely, but he who makes his ways crooked will be found out" (Proverbs 10:9, ESV). Trustworthy character brings security to your life, relationships, and organization. If you want to build enduring influence, put the pencil in God's hands, and make trustworthy character your foundation.

3) Inspiring Vision

Many years ago, I attended a conference at Saddleback Valley Community Church in Orange County, California. The event was great, and it delivered practical and inspirational content. But one session impacted me the most—and I don't even remember what was said.

Rick Warren, the pastor of Saddleback at the time, taught a session where he cast vision for small group ministry. All these years later, I don't remember his points, and I don't remember his illustrations, but I do remember how I *felt*.

Inspired.

Hopeful.

Motivated.

Moved to my core.

When the session concluded, I walked out of the building to my rental car in the parking lot. I didn't leave the conference. I didn't take a nap in the warm California sun. And I didn't review my notes from the session.

I sat in my car and wept.

Had I just received bad news? No!

Was I angry because somebody had hurt me? Nope!

With tears in my eyes, I repented for dreaming too small.

Pastor Rick's vision inspired me so much that I realized I had been playing it safe. I thought too small. I risked too little. I dreamed too ordinarily. My cause was too comfortable. I had put God in a box, and that day I let Him out. I asked Him to forgive me, and then I invited the Holy Spirit to stretch my mind and inspire fresh vision in my heart.

Your vision flows out of your personal calling, and then it engages the people around you. That's what happened to Paul. He was called to reach the Gentiles with the gospel, and he even told King Agrippa, "I obeyed that vision from heaven" (Acts 26:19). But then his personal calling produced an inspiring vision that engaged others.

For example, Timothy and Epaphroditus became partners with Paul in the proclamation of the gospel. Epaphroditus even risked his life for the cause of Christ (Philippians 2:20, 30). Paul had other co-laborers too—Barnabas, Apollos, Aquilla, Titus, Luke, and Silas, just to name a few. "Depending upon how broadly the term is defined, eighty to ninety people are described as Paul's co-workers."[67]

Paul also enlisted prayer partners in his vision. He wrote to the Colossians:

Pray for us, too, that God will give us many opportunities to speak about his mysterious plan concerning Christ. That is why I am here in chains. Pray that I will proclaim this message as clearly as I should. —Colossians 4:3-4

Paul's vision wasn't a solo endeavor. It was a cause that attracted a cohort of faithful leaders.

Vision is a powerful picture of a preferred future, and good leaders know how to inspire a shared vision among the people they lead. Where does it begin? In my experience, it requires four keys.

Credibility. Before people enthusiastically pursue a vision, they must first believe in the credibility of the leader. John Maxwell calls it "The Law of Buy-In: People buy into the leader, then the vision."[68] Big visions without equally big buy-in produce little progress. People will throw their resources behind your vision when they can throw their confidence behind you.

Collaboration. Based on their extensive research, authors James Kouzes and Barry Posner noted, "Too many people think that it's the leader's job to develop the vision when the reality is that people want to be involved in this process. You can't command commitment; you have to inspire it."[69] Start the visioning process with personal prayer, reflection, and dreaming, but once you get snapshots of the future, invite a core group of leaders to provide feedback and perspective. Without collaboration, vision is *seen* but not *shared*.

Courage. In the movie *Braveheart*, William Wallace announces that he will invade England and defeat the English on their own ground. His audience scoffed, "That's impossible." But Wallace pushed back:

"Why? Why is that impossible? You're so concerned with squabbling for the scraps from Longshank's table that you've missed your God-given right to something better. There is a difference between us. You think the people of this country exist to provide you with possession. I think your possession exists to provide those people with freedom. And I go to make sure that they have it."

When Robert the Bruce follows Wallace out of the gathering, he says, "I respect what you said, but remember that these men have lands and castles. It's much to risk." He warns Wallace that if he makes enemies on both sides of the border, he'll end up dead.

Wallace replies, "We all end up dead; it's just a question of how and why." Then, he challenges Robert the Bruce with what it means to be noble: "Your title gives you claim to the throne of our country, but men don't follow titles, they follow courage. Now our people know you. Noble, and common, they respect you. And if you would just lead them to freedom, they'd follow you. And so would I."[70]

Positions and titles are important to us, but they're no big deal to the people we lead. People follow courage, not titles. As Billy Graham once said, "Courage is contagious. When a brave man takes a stand, the spines of others are often stiffened."[71] You can't inspire vision in others if you lack the courage to pursue a dream bigger than yourself.

Communication. Once the vision comes into focus, communicate it clearly, frequently, and passionately. If your vision is unclear, it will create uncertainty for everyone else. If you don't communicate the vision frequently, it will be nothing more than a singular ambition rather than a shared dream. And if you fail to communicate your vision passionately, you'll bore your audience to tears. That day, in Southern California, Rick Warren exuded a contagious passion. I simply could not ignore his infectious vision.

Influence is a trust given to us by God. If we don't use our influence to make things better, one day, we'll have no more influence. It requires an inspiring vision that others can rally behind to make the world a better place.

4) Proven Competence

It's one thing to have an inspiring vision, but it's quite another to turn that vision into reality. This is where competence plays a critical role. Competence is only proven when it delivers the intended results.

Paul's competence—and its direct impact on his influence—is evident throughout his life. Before his encounter with Jesus, Paul's competence was based on his heritage as a "pure-blooded citizen of Israel and a member of the tribe of Benjamin" (Philippians 3:5). Furthermore, Paul came from the influential city of Tarsus, shaped by its size, bustling commerce, political power, and educational standing.[72] And finally, Paul excelled in his education and career, trained under the best of the best, Gamaliel, the grandson of Hillel (Acts 22:3). Author John Pollock observed, "Paul's father could take full and justified delight in this son who had followed in his steps as a Pharisee and had the intellectual force to reach the highest office in Israel."[73] Before Paul's conversion to Christ, his competence—informed by his heritage, education, citizenship, and position as a Pharisee—powered his influence (see Philippians 3:4-6).

However, after Jesus intercepted Paul's life on the road to Damascus, his competence was defined by the tangible impact he had on people's lives. Paul said to the Christians in Corinth, "Your lives are a letter written in our hearts; everyone can read it and recognize our good work among you. Clearly, you are a letter from Christ showing the result of our ministry among you" (2 Corinthians 3:2-3). Paul didn't need anybody's endorsement letter to substantiate his ministry. Instead, the transformation in the Corinthian believers' lives validated his competence and impact. And who made this possible? Paul said, "Our qualification comes from God" (v. 5).

We also see Paul's competence expressed through his communication skills. In Acts 17, Paul was troubled by the sight of idols in the city of Athens, so "he went to the synagogue to reason with the Jews and the God-fearing Gentiles, and he spoke daily in the public square to all who happened to be there" (v. 17). And when he debated with some of the Epicurean and Stoic philosophers, they said, "Come and tell us about this new teaching ... we want to know what it's all about" (vv. 19-20). Debate wasn't a means to antagonize these philosophers. After all, they spent their time "discussing the latest ideas" (v. 21). Instead, Paul used his communication skills to present the gospel, and it worked. While people laughed at Paul when he explained the resurrection of Jesus, "some joined him and became believers" (v. 34).

Finally, Paul was a competent tentmaker, church planter, mentor, and writer. In His wisdom and sovereignty, God used each of Paul's skills to take new territory for the cause of Christ.

The same will be true for you. Your competence plays an important role in your ability to gain influence for a cause that's bigger than yourself. To improve your leadership competence, put these tips to work:

- Embrace a teachable mindset.
- Take assessments to raise your awareness of your strengths and weaknesses.
- Seek feedback from trusted leaders to help you address your leadership blind spots.
- Create a growth plan to develop your leadership competencies.
- Secure a leadership coach to help you grow.
- Become proficient in leadership skills through regular practice.
- Lean into your greatest gifts to make your largest impact.

As your competence grows, more people will trust you to lead them. They'll say, "Not only does she possess an inspiring vision, but I'm confident she has the ability to lead us there." They'll say, "Not only does he model trustworthy character, but I believe he has the capacity to take the organization to the next level." Competence increases influence.

5) Relational Investment

The final ingredient to building influence is *Relational Investment*. This was the rocket booster that thrust Paul's influence well beyond his immediate reach. It's especially clear in Paul's relationship with Timothy, his "true son in the faith" (1 Timothy 1:2).

In his second letter to Timothy, Paul wrote, "You have heard me teach things that have been confirmed by many reliable witnesses. Now teach these truths to other trustworthy people who will be able to pass them on to others" (2 Timothy 2:2). Not only did Paul invest in Timothy's life, but he commissioned Timothy to do the same with others. Embedded in Paul's instruction is the power of multiplication. Once Timothy taught foundational truths to "trustworthy people," they were to "pass them on to others."

Why was Paul able to empower Timothy with these instructions? Because he built a relationship with Timothy and invested in his life. They took missionary journeys together. They had countless conversations about life and the gospel. And, in both of his letters to Timothy, Paul equipped him with very specific instructions. He even said, "Timothy, my son, here are my instructions for you, based on the prophetic words spoken about you earlier. May they help you fight well in the Lord's battles" (1 Timothy 1:18).

Relational investment wasn't a practice reserved for the apostle Paul. We can put it to work today through three influence-building expressions: connection, compassion, and coaching.

Connection. Relational investment begins when you connect with the people you lead. People skills—such as authenticity, respect, attentiveness, kindness, and etiquette—will build relational equity. The people you'll influence the most are those with whom you have the deepest relationship. Connection is the starting point.

Compassion. Relationships are more than transactional interactions—if you do *this* for me, I'll do *that* for you. People don't want to feel used; they want to feel *known* and *noticed*. Care trumps efficiency in leadership. When we show compassion, we demonstrate to the people we lead how much we care about them as people. We take an interest in their lives and their families. We rejoice in their wins and mourn their losses. We celebrate their victories and walk with them through their valleys. Building influence isn't the reason we show compassion—it's just the natural by-product of being a caring and compassionate person.

Coaching. The final level of relational investment happens when we coach the people we lead. As I noted in chapter 4, there's a big difference between achievers and high-capacity leaders. One focuses on tasks while the other focuses on people. One is a *doer*, and the other is a *developer*. High-capacity leaders make people development their highest priority. They see the potential in others, help them see it in themselves, and then coach, equip, and empower them to reach it. That's what Paul did with Timothy. If you want to maximize your relational investment, help your team members grow. (We'll unpack a powerful coaching model in chapter 12.)

WHAT DIFFERENCE WILL YOU MAKE WITH YOUR INFLUENCE?

Let me close with one important challenge: don't seek influence for the sake of influence. Influence is simply the by-product of who you are and what you do. When you attune your life to a personal calling, model trustworthy character, possess an inspiring vision, exercise competence, and invest in relationships, your influence will naturally grow. Focus on the inputs and trust God with the influence.

> **The real question isn't about how much influence you have, but rather, what will you do with the influence God has entrusted to you?**

Authors Ken Blanchard and Mark Miller observed, "Anytime you influence the thinking, beliefs, or development of another person, you're engaging in leadership."[74] The real question isn't about how much influence you have, but rather, what will you do with the influence God has entrusted to you?

In the beginning, Paul used his influence to produce fear and inflict pain, suffering, and death. But after an encounter with Jesus, he turned the world upside down for the cause of the gospel (Acts 7:16). What about you? What difference will you make with your influence? To make your greatest impact, answer these five questions:

- What need can I meet?
- What problem can I solve?
- What person can I help?
- What beauty can I create?
- What disciple can I make?

Your answers to those questions will reveal how you can leverage your influence for the greatest good. When you meet real needs, solve painful problems, help hurting people, create God-honoring beauty, and make disciples of Jesus, your influence brings glory to God.

All of us exhibit greater strength in one influence-building ingredient over another. Your character might be great, but your vision may be unclear. Your competence may deliver outstanding results, but your investment in relationships may be average. If you're going to build enduring influence for the good of others and the glory of God, you need all five ingredients. To help you get started, use Leadership Tool #7: Influence Builder.

INSANELY PRACTICAL REFLECTION AND DISCUSSION

1. Who are one or two people you would include in your "top influencers" list that have significantly impacted your life?
2. Which of the five keys to building influence was missing when a leader or coworker tried to build influence with you? How did you respond? What lessons can you learn from that encounter?
3. Which of the five influence-building keys do you need to give more attention to—personal calling, trustworthy character, inspiring vision, proven competence, or relational investment? What would be a good first step to grow in this area?
4. What difference do you want to make with the influence God has entrusted to you?

LEADERSHIP TOOL #7
Influence Builder

Building influence requires five keys: Personal Calling, Trustworthy Character, Inspiring Vision, Proven Competence, and Relational Investment. Answer the questions under each ingredient below to help you create a practical plan to build enduring, God-honoring influence.

INFLUENCE-BUILDING PLAN	
PERSONAL CALLING	
1. Have you responded to Jesus's call to surrender to Him, receive His grace, and follow His lead?	
2. What is God's calling for your life (those "good works" He created and gifted you to do)?	
TRUSTWORTHY CHARACTER	
1. What two areas of your character and integrity do you need to focus on growing the most?	
2. What steps will you take to grow these character traits in the next thirty days, and who can hold you accountable?	
INSPIRING VISION	
1. Describe your courageous vision. How can your team collaborate with you to bring your vision into focus?	
2. What steps will you take to communicate your vision to your team, department, or organization?	

PROVEN COMPETENCE	
1. What are your strongest and weakest leadership skills? If you don't know, what trusted leader can you ask?	
2. How can you develop a growth plan and lean on your growth team to develop these leadership skills?	
RELATIONAL INVESTMENT	
1. How can you connect regularly with your team and show greater compassion to your team members?	
2. Who are three people you can begin coaching to help them cultivate their leadership potential?	
USING YOUR INFLUENCE TO MAKE A DIFFERENCE	
How will you use your influence to: 1) Meet a need, 2) Solve a problem, 3) Help a person, 4) Create beauty, or 5) Make a disciple of Jesus?	

Download the Influence Builder tool at insanelypracticalleadership.com.

CHAPTER 8

HOW TO LEAD PEOPLE

"Leadership: The skill of influencing people to work enthusiastically toward goals identified as being for the common good."
—James Hunter

One of the greatest leadership feats of the twentieth century was Sir Ernest Shackleton's Imperial Trans-Antarctic Expedition. The goal of the expedition was clear: cross the continent of Antarctica from west to east. From the five thousand applications that flooded Shackleton's office for this monumental voyage, he chose fifty-six men—twenty-eight for the Weddell Sea party to sail on *Endurance* and twenty-eight to sail on the *Aurora* to station supplies along the polar route.[75] In the end, Shackleton's greatest leadership feat wasn't the crossing of Antarctica but winning a two-year wrestling match to survive its ice-cold death grip.

Shackleton spent nearly two years raising funds for the expedition before the *Endurance* finally set sail. The ship was named after Shackleton's family motto, *Fortitudine Vincimus*—"By endurance we conquer." The crew departed London on Saturday, August 1, 1914, from the West India Dock. After making a stop in Buenos Aires, they set sail again on October 26 for the eleven-day journey to South Georgia where they would collect supplies before heading to the Antarctic coast.[76] Unbeknownst to Shackleton, *Endurance* would be an appropriate name for the unforeseen journey ahead.

Norwegian whalers warned Shackleton against sailing to Antarctica, insisting it was far too dangerous. Shackleton ignored them, embarking on the journey to his destination on December 5. But after only a few days of favorable weather, they encountered ice packs. The ship's captain, Frank Worsley, did his best to navigate the floes and icebergs, but sixty miles from their destination, everything came to a halt. They were trapped by the ice floe.[77] Thomas Orde-Lees, the storekeeper on board, described the ship as "frozen, like an almond in the middle of a chocolate bar."[78]

Months passed as the ship remained wedged in a sea of ice, and then, in early May, the sun disappeared from the sky. Darkness covered Antarctica for the next seventy-nine days and temperatures that June averaged -17 degrees.[79] Yet, despite the dark sky, the crew maintained a strangely bright outlook—until the end of August. That's when the *Endurance* cracked and groaned as the pressure of the floe tested its strength.

In the weeks ahead, ice began to grind against the stern. Captain Worsley lowered the lifeboats, and the crew removed essential gear from the ship. Then, on October 27, 1915, Shackleton gave orders to abandon ship. Twenty-five days later, *Endurance* was gone—crushed and swallowed by the ice.

PATIENCE CAMP

"The Boss"—as Shackleton was known—planned to march to Paulet Island, 346 miles away, pulling lifeboats weighing more than a ton through the ice. But the attempt was exhausting and unattainable, not to mention crazy. They gave up after traveling only nine miles in five days.[80]

Within a few weeks, they set up "Patience Camp," a prophetic name for the long months ahead as they patiently navigated the shifting floe. The conditions were brutal. When the men had to relieve themselves, ice became their toilet paper. When their eyes watered, tears rolled down their faces and froze on the tips of their noses. To make matters worse, food was sparse. The dreadful day came when they had to shoot their dogs just so they could eat. And time moved painfully slow. Monotony plagued the men as days turned into weeks and then into months.[81]

The unpredictable ice floe moved in one direction and then shifted erratically as the currents changed. The swell of the ocean caused the floe to rise and then dip like rolling hills. The constant movement took its toll, and the floe began to crack and split.

Finally, on April 9, the Boss gave the order: "Launch the boats." Immediately, the men thrust three lifeboats into the water—the *James Caird*, the *Dudley Docker*, and the *Stancomb Wills*. The *Caird* was named after Sir James Caird, an eleventh-hour generous donor to the expedition. The *Dudley Docker* was christened in honor of a British industrialist, and the *Stancomb Wills* was named after a British tobacco heiress, Janet Stancomb-Wills.[82] With the rapid launch of the boats, the men vacated Patience Camp.

For a week, the crew made a perilous, sleepless journey through the violent ocean with the constant threat of whales, floes, and icebergs. Even though the men rowed as hard as they could, strong undercurrents reversed their course and pulled them in the wrong direction. Gale force winds battered the boats, the crew's clothes were cold and wet, and physical and emotional exhaustion plagued them. If their situation wasn't bad enough, most of the men also had diarrhea. But thankfully, after a heroic effort, the men made landfall on Elephant Island on April 15, 1916.

ELEPHANT ISLAND

The men were dead tired—shivering, exhausted, and frostbitten. While the rugged terrain of Elephant Island was remote, frigid, and home to nothing more than penguins and elephant seals, the crew finally stood on solid ground. However, it didn't take the Boss long to announce the inevitable: five men would join him and set sail in the *James Caird* for South Georgia in hopes of returning with a ship to collect the rest of the men. Every man volunteered to go, but Shackleton selected Tom Crean, Henry McNeish, John Vincent, Timothy McCarthy, and, of course, the expert navigator, Captain Frank Worsley.

The largest lifeboat—the *James Caird* at twenty-two feet six inches long—was prepared and reinforced for sailing. Then, on April 24, 1916, the Boss and his small crew said farewell, leaving his second in command, Frank Wild, in charge of the other twenty-one men. Standing on the coastline, the men waved goodbye until the *James Caird* disappeared from the horizon. They knew they may never see Shackleton and the crew again.

In the days that followed, the men on Elephant Island built a small hut with the two remaining boats and their meager supplies. Winter descended on the island with a wallop as blizzard conditions pounded the hut. Each day, members of the team ascended a hill, looking with hopeful anticipation for any sign of a rescue ship. But time and again, they returned with somber faces of defeat. Maybe tomorrow.

While they did their best to remain steadfast in the face of bone-chilling temperatures and life-threatening circumstances, two of the men became incapacitated. Perce Blackborow suffered extreme frostbite, and James McIlroy, one of the physicians among the group, had to amputate his foot. The surgery lasted fifty-five minutes as McIlroy cut off each toe and then scraped away the dead flesh.[83] Then, near the end of July, McIlroy drained more than two pints of fluid from an abscess the size of a football on Hubert Hudson's buttock.[84] Though nobody would verbalize it, each passing day—which turned into weeks and then months— dampened the hopes that Shackleton would survive the journey to South Georgia.

THE VOYAGE TO SOUTH GEORGIA

The ocean was cruel and tumultuous. When the South Georgia-bound crew left Elephant Island, the men rotated in four-hour shifts, watching for the danger of ice. By April 26, the small six-man team entered the Drake Passage, 128 miles from Elephant Island. Affectionately known as the "Drake Shake," this inhospitable and unbridled six-hundred-mile-wide body of water is over eleven thousand feet deep. And the latitudes of forty to sixty generate vicious winds nicknamed the "roaring forties," "furious fifties," and "screaming sixties."[85]

In the "Drake Shake," the men were thrashed and ragged. Their fingers were frostbitten, and saltwater boils covered their wrists, ankles, and buttocks.[86] Ice encased the entire boat above the waterline—a half-foot thick in some places—and they took turns beating ice off the oars and the boat.[87] On one occasion, a large wave hit the *Caird,* and the crew spent two hours pumping knee-deep water out of the boat.[88] Furthermore, their reindeer sleeping bags began to rot and reek with stench. And to make matters even more dire, sea water seeped into their second cask of fresh water—the only water they had left to drink.[89]

And yet, against all odds, Shackleton's optimism infected his crew, and on May 10, 1916, they reached the island. It had been 522 days since they originally left South Georgia, but here they were, standing on the shore once again—this time on the opposite side of the island from the Stromness whaling station.[90] Then, they sailed six more miles to the head of King Haakon Bay, hauled the *Caird* onto the beach, and formulated a plan to reach their final destination.

The battered lifeboat couldn't sail another 130 miles to the whaling station. There was only one daunting, unnerving option—scale the ten thousand-foot mountains in front of them. They waited for a clear moon, twisted brass screws into the soles of their shoes to give them traction on the ice, and then set off on foot. Though they stopped for a brief rest every twenty minutes, the men kept climbing and refused to quit.[91]

Finally, the Boss heard the faint sound of a whistle. Their spirits revived. The hope of salvation called in the distance. Mustering every ounce of strength remaining, they completed the thirty-six-hour trek and reached the Stromness whaling station. When they arrived, nobody recognized them. After nearly two years, Shackleton and his men were back from the dead.

That day, each man enjoyed a hot bath, a change of clothes, and a warm meal. While they gladly welcomed these scarce comforts, the Boss refused to relax his rescue efforts. After all, the best leaders look out for their team members—every last one of them.

In the following months, Shackleton made three fearless attempts to reach the twenty-two men waiting on Elephant Island, but each effort failed, obstructed by the impenetrable ice. Finally, on the fourth attempt, aboard a sea-going tug called the *Yelcho*, Elephant Island came into view. It was August 30, 1916—one-hundred and twenty-eight days since the Boss departed the island in search of South Georgia.[92]

But there they were.

Shackleton held his breath as he counted.

One, two, three.

Nine, ten, eleven.

Twenty, twenty-one ... twenty-two.

Relief swept across his face. Every man was alive, standing on the shore waving at the oncoming ship.[93] With relief and gratitude, the men boarded the boat, and the journey home began.

HOW TO LEAD PEOPLE

Author James Hunter defines leadership: "The skill of influencing people to work enthusiastically toward goals identified as being for the common good."[94] And that's what Sir Ernest Shackleton did in a monumental way during a perilous two-year journey. Though you're likely not taking a journey to Antarctica anytime soon, I want to point out eight lessons we can glean from the Boss. These lessons are the crux of what it looks like to lead people.

1) Vision: Communicate an inspiring picture of the future

When Shackleton posted a sign outside his office at No. 4 New Burlington Street advertising an upcoming Imperial Trans-Antarctic Expedition, his vision was clear: cross the continent of Antarctica from west to east. He further promoted his vision on December 29, 1913, in a letter to *The Times* in London. That vision inspired nearly five thousand people to submit applications for this extraordinary adventure.

The lesson is clear: vision matters. People won't follow you if you can't take them somewhere better or more inspiring than where they are right now. Vision is the great motivator that catalyzes people to do more than they've ever done and go further than they've ever gone. Before you lead people, you better know where you're going.

As I noted in the last chapter, having a cause bigger than yourself is one of the keys to building influence. It's also essential when unexpected setbacks arise along the way. Vision defines a true north to guide the team no matter what hardships may come. Here are a few questions to help you clarify your vision:

- What dream is the Holy Spirit birthing inside you?
- What need are we best equipped to meet?
- What problem can we uniquely solve?
- Where do we envision being two years from now?
- What have I been dreaming about lately that I can't seem to shake?
- What new opportunities have come on the horizon?
- What audacious goal is calling out to us?
- What organizational growth engine should we leverage for greater impact?

Answering these questions will help you identify your vision for the future. As you gain clarity, share your ideas with an inner circle of leaders to get their perspective and refine the vision. As you do, the vision will become crystal clear. Then, heed the wisdom of Habakkuk 2:2: "Write down the vision; write it clearly on clay tablets so whoever reads it can run to tell others" (NCV).

> **Sometimes, you'll be forced to make tweaks to your vision or alter your original plans. That's okay.**

You might read this and say, "But Shackleton didn't achieve his vision." I would argue he didn't achieve his *original* vision. But he did achieve the most important vision: to get his entire crew safely home. And he made that vision abundantly clear. After the ice swallowed the *Endurance*, the Boss pulled his men together, served them hot tea, and then confidently said, "Ship and stores have gone, so now we'll go home."[95] Imagine hearing those words when you don't even have a ship to sail home.

Sometimes, you'll be forced to make tweaks to your vision or alter your original plans. That's okay. Only in extreme cases will you have to "go home." However, jumping erratically from one vision to another will result in organizational whiplash and leave your team feeling exasperated. Make the vision clear, and then stick to it.

2) Strategy: Create a path forward

Every *vision* requires a *strategy* to seize it. Without strategy, visionary leaders will devolve into nothing more than hallucinating dreamers. Strategy creates a path for the vision to move out of our imagination and into reality. In fact, strategy breaks the vision into smaller, bite-sized goals with clear action steps to move you systematically closer to the vision.

Shackleton's original strategy to fulfill his trans-Antarctic vision involved two ships, specific polar routes, and detailed action plans. The first ship, *Endurance*, would land at Vahsel Bay in the Weddell Sea to make the trek across the pole. They would cover 1,500 miles in one hundred days—an ambitious pace of fifteen miles per day. The second ship, *Aurora*, would land at McMurdo Sound in the Ross Sea to station supplies along the route to sustain the crew.[96]

Because Shackleton's original vision was thwarted, he was forced to adopt a new strategy—one that would get the crew safely home. Therein lies an important lesson: plans rarely go as planned. Leaders must manage the tension between *focus* and *flexibility* to create a strategy to achieve what matters most.

> **Creating a strategy shouldn't be done in a silo.**

Some leaders are great at charting a course to seize what they see. Others are amazing dreamers, but they don't have a strategizing bone in their body. If that's you, team up with a strategist. Find someone who loves putting legs on bold visions. Either way, your strategy needs to address five areas:

- **Reality**—Diagnose your organizational reality by identifying the strengths and opportunities you can leverage for the vision and the weaknesses and obstacles you'll need to overcome.
- **Research**—Do your homework to identify the best practices and pathways to achieve the vision. Embrace a learning posture, glean insights from industry experts, and do the hard work to formulate a solid path forward.
- **Resources**—Identify the resources you will need to achieve the vision. Your resources will include money, people, time, and tools. You may not have all the resources you need; therefore, be sure your strategy addresses these gaps.
- **Roadmap**—Create a clear roadmap to the vision that's deeply informed by your reality, research, and resources. Your roadmap should establish clear goals, steps to reach the goals, and who will own each goal.
- **Rollout**—Determine how to roll out the strategy to the entire organization with clear communication and appropriate next steps.

Creating a strategy shouldn't be done in a silo. Instead, involve others in the process by maximizing the strengths of your team. This will result in a better strategy as well as greater levels of buy-in.

3) Team Expectations: Define roles and goals

When five thousand applications flooded Shackleton's office for his Antarctic expedition, he did the tedious work of selecting the right men for the job. Teamwork, loyalty, optimism, and hard work were immensely important to Shackleton, as was a guiding principle he gleaned from a London theatrical manager who once told him, "Character and temperament matter quite as much as acting ability."[97]

With each team member he assembled, the Boss gave them a clear role to play. Frank Wild was second-in-command, and Frank Worsley was the captain of the ship. Then, there was the navigator, Hubert Hudson, and the photographer, Frank Hurley. There were also three officers, two surgeons, two engineers, a biologist, a meteorologist, a geologist, a physicist, an artist, a storekeeper, a carpenter, a cook, a steward, a dog handler, firemen, and able seamen. Each man had a role to play and a goal to achieve that kept them engaged in the larger vision.

Each person you lead also needs a *clear role* and a *specific goal*. Your job is to define the role. Their job is to define the goal.

For the role, create a written role description that articulates their position on the team, who they report to, who reports to them, the expectations of the role, and their unique responsibilities. This important tool makes your expectations painstakingly clear.

For the goals, let each team member choose their own. This will increase buy-in and create ownership. However, you should have the final say to ensure each person's goals are aligned with their responsibilities and the organization's highest priorities.

Roles and goals need two keys to be effective: clarity and accountability. You'll establish clarity when the role and goal are put in writing, and you'll maintain accountability by conducting regular one-on-one meetings with each team member to encourage and coach them toward success.

4) Equipping: Prepare the team to succeed

You can't do a job without the right tools, and Shackleton provided the very best for his crew. He had no patience for inadequate or poorly made tools. Thomas Orde-Lees, the storekeeper for the *Endurance*, wrote:

Every regard was made to the protection of life and limb and the general health of the party, unlimited attention was given to the all important matter of diet, and the polar equipment and scientific instruments were all of the latest type and well nigh perfect; in fact nothing was left to chance except the ice, a factor which no amount of provision could regulate.[98]

The Boss knew his crew wouldn't succeed unless he equipped them to do so.

The same is true for you. One of the best ways to invest in the people you lead is to equip them for service. In fact, the apostle Paul defined equipping as the primary purpose of leaders in the church. He said, "Their responsibility is to equip God's people to do his work and build up the church, the body of Christ" (Ephesians 4:12).

Equipping is multidimensional. It helps people grow and prepares them to lead. A great way to equip the members of your team is to implement the TREC method:

- **T**raining—Equip the people you lead with the training to excel at their role. This training might happen in a classroom or workshop, with a helpful resource, or through a course, curriculum, or digital platform.
- **R**esources—In the same way a pilot can't do his job without an airplane, the members of your team can't do their job

without the tools and resources necessary to achieve intended objectives. Carefully select those resources and put them into the hands of your team.
- **Experience**—Whether it's through stretch assignments or opportunities to get their feet wet, lead your team into the trenches where they can acquire the experience to become proficient at their role. Experience applies training and resources.
- **Coaching**—Some of the best equipping happens when people are teamed up with coaches and mentors. This provides personalized instruction, observation, encouragement, and the opportunity to ask questions.

You'll reduce frustration and accelerate progress if you equip people with the TREC method. Once the team is equipped, be sure to take the next step.

5) Delegation: Empower the team to act

Shackleton had a high standard, but he wasn't a micromanager. Perhaps his greatest expression of empowered delegation happened when he put Frank Wild in charge of the men who remained on Elephant Island while Shackleton and a small crew journeyed to South Georgia. The Boss had great confidence in Wild, convinced he could hold the men together as they endured the ruthless conditions. His conviction proved true. The men survived the brutal winter during Shackleton's four-month absence, and they greeted the Boss with enthusiastic waves when his ship appeared on the horizon.

You can equip your team all day long, but at some point, you must delegate responsibility and release power. When Jethro, the father-in-law of Moses, instructed him to create a sustainable structure to manage his leadership load, Moses took his advice to heart: "He chose capable men from all over Israel and appointed them as leaders over the people. He put them in charge of groups of one thousand, one hundred, fifty, and ten" (Exodus 18:25, emphasis added). Moses didn't just select a team; he "put them in charge." Recruitment and empowerment were part of the equation. Effective delegation requires the four As:

- **Assignment**—Begin by identifying the assignments to delegate to members of your team. Above all, be sure each assignment is aligned with their giftedness.
- **Authority**—Give team members the authority to make decisions. Without authority, they'll feel micromanaged by the constant need to get your approval before they can act.
- **Accountability**—When you give away authority, you must also hold team members accountable to deliver results. If you do a good job equipping your team, there's a far greater likelihood they'll produce desired outcomes.
- **Affirmation**—Be sure to give the team plenty of encouragement along the way. Affirmation is the fuel that engages the heart.

This is your delegation roadmap. It will help you not only release responsibility to others, but it will fully empower them to excel.

6) Collaboration: Foster relationships, cooperation, and unity

Authors Margot Morrell and Stephanie Capparell observed of Shackleton, "On the *Endurance*, he focused on the one thing that gave him the best chance at reaching his goals: unity."[99] One way he did this was by eliminating hierarchical structures.

For example, Shackleton balanced the work of the scientists and the seamen by having them help each other. The scientists helped with the ship's chores, and the seamen helped by taking scientific readings and samples. In addition, each crew member took turns sailing, doing night watch, caring for the dogs, and scrubbing floors.[100] Shackleton also rotated work assignments, so the men could build friendships as they served alongside each crew member.[101] Furthermore, the Boss insisted the men spend no more than a week sharing a tent with the same man. This would eliminate cliques and any brewing conflicts.[102]

Fighting for the unity of your team is paramount. Paul implored the early church, "Live in harmony with each other" and "be of one mind, united in thought and purpose" (1 Corinthians 1:10). When unity is present, relationships flourish, decisions are made faster, and frankly, everything is more fun. Three simple tactics will bolster your efforts to create a unified team.

First, focus on relationship building. People are more patient and engaged with coworkers when a strong relationship undergirds their interactions. These relationships form when there's opportunity to work together in small groups and when the team can have fun together outside of work. Shackleton employed both tactics.

Second, collaborate on projects. It's easy to dole out tasks and assign projects to individuals, but when the entire team collaborates on a project, it creates a unifying focus. For example, each quarter, our team works together on one big goal that unifies our efforts. It's invigorating as we watch a long list of action steps turn from red to yellow to green as the team works hard to achieve this shared objective. It also creates a great point of celebration when the goal is finally realized.

Third, nip divisiveness in the bud. Divisive attitudes have a way of multiplying quickly. When you smell a hint of division, deal with it quickly. Don't let it brew because you're too afraid to confront it. This requires some hard conversations, but it's essential for the long-term unity of the team.

> **Compassion for the people you lead matters. You're not just doing tasks, counting numbers, and balancing budgets. You're leading human beings—people with hearts, emotions, families, hopes, dreams, and fears.**

7) Compassion: Show people you care

Shackleton cared deeply for his crew, and he did his best to show it in personal and collective ways. For example, when *Endurance* was trapped in the ice, he kept the spirits of the crew high by requiring them to come together for conversation, games, and occasional contests following dinner. He believed this was essential to ward off worry, despair, and moral collapse.[103]

The crew also played sports like soccer and ice hockey, observed holidays, celebrated birthdays, and enjoyed sing-alongs as

Leonard Hussey played his five-string banjo. Shackleton believed Hussey's banjo was "vital mental medicine" and would prove essential to maintaining the morale of the crew and fending off symptoms of depression.[104] On top of all of this, each day, even during blizzards, the Boss visited each tent to inquire about every man's health and comfort.[105]

Compassion for the people you lead matters. You're not just doing tasks, counting numbers, and balancing budgets. You're leading human beings—people with hearts, emotions, families, hopes, dreams, and fears. The apostle Peter's wisdom is particularly important to keep in mind:

> *Care for the flock that God has entrusted to you. Watch over it willingly, not grudgingly—not for what you will get out of it, but because you are eager to serve God. Don't lord it over the people assigned to your care, but lead them by your own good example. —1 Peter 5:2-3*

You may be naturally relational and highly extroverted. Or you may be more like me—introverted and task-oriented. So, how should you practically care for the people you lead? Here are a few tips.

- Ask how they're doing personally.
- Inquire about their family.
- Give them your undivided attention.
- Make the rounds to check on your team.
- Celebrate their birthday and work anniversary.
- Compliment them publicly.
- Listen to their feedback.
- Ask, "How can I help?"
- Send a thank you card or text.

- Surprise them with coffee, donuts, or a gift card.
- Take them to lunch.
- Pray *for* them and *with* them.
- Invite them to be your guest at a special event.
- Plan a fun team outing.
- Give them a bonus or a raise.
- Invest in their growth.
- Show them grace.

None of these tips are rocket science, but all of them require intentionality. Be deliberate in your efforts to care for the people you lead.

8) Communication: Keep people in the know

Three qualities marked Shackleton's communication: honesty, optimism, and regularity. He kept the crew in the know as the unpredictable situation evolved. He didn't hide the hard facts, but he also maintained an indomitable optimism. After losing the ship, the Boss gathered the group and shared a heartfelt speech, thanking them for their support and giving detailed plans of what they would do next. Leonard Hussey, the crew's meteorologist, later wrote, "It was a characteristic speech—simple, moving, optimistic and highly effective. It brought us out of our doldrums, our spirits rose, and we had our supper."[106]

When you're communicating with the people you lead, keep in mind the three Fs: Facts, Feelings, and Frequency. First, keep your communication factual, never exaggerating the truth or hiding information your team needs to do their job. Second, communicate with feeling (passion and belief) and with regard to *their* feelings (being aware of your tone and how you come across to others). Third, make your communication frequent. It's easy to assume people know what's in our heads, but that assumption is misguided at best. Regularly communicate with your team and keep them in the know.

These eight keys will help you lead people. Think about the alternative. Do you really believe you'll succeed with a foggy vision, undeveloped strategy, unclear expectations, poorly equipped and empowered team members, disunity, a lack of compassion, and poor communication? There are certainly other keys to effective leadership, but these eight will put you on the path to success. To assess each key and to develop a plan for improvement, implement Leadership Tool #8: Skills to Leading Well.

INSANELY PRACTICAL REFLECTION AND DISCUSSION

1. How does Sir Ernest Shackleton's leadership inspire you?
2. How have you seen the eight leadership skills leveraged for extraordinary impact in your leadership circles?
3. Which of the eight leadership skills is the hardest one for you to master? Why?
4. Which practical tips in this chapter can you immediately implement to more effectively lead people?

LEADERSHIP TOOL #8
Skills to Leading Well

Use the Leading Well chart below to assess yourself in each leadership skill and to develop a plan to improve.

SKILLS TO LEADING WELL	
Give yourself a score on a scale from 1 to 10 (10 being the best) in each leadership skill below. Then, reflect on the ideas and insights in this chapter to create a simple plan to improve.	
VISION: COMMUNICATE AN INSPIRING PICTURE OF THE FUTURE	
SCORE (1-10)	IMPROVEMENT PLAN:
STRATEGY: CREATE A PATH FORWARD	
SCORE (1-10)	IMPROVEMENT PLAN:
TEAM EXPECTATIONS: DEFINE ROLES AND GOALS	
SCORE (1-10)	IMPROVEMENT PLAN:
EQUIPPING: PREPARE THE TEAM TO SUCCEED	
SCORE (1-10)	IMPROVEMENT PLAN:
DELEGATION: EMPOWER THE TEAM TO ACT	
SCORE (1-10)	IMPROVEMENT PLAN:

COLLABORATION: FOSTER RELATIONSHIPS, COOPERATION, and UNITY	
SCORE (1-10)	IMPROVEMENT PLAN:

COMPASSION: SHOW PEOPLE YOU CARE	
SCORE (1-10)	IMPROVEMENT PLAN:

COMMUNICATION: KEEP PEOPLE IN THE KNOW	
SCORE (1-10)	IMPROVEMENT PLAN:

Download the Skills to Leading Well tool at insanelypracticalleadership.com.

CHAPTER 9

HOW TO BE A SERVANT LEADER

"The best way to find out whether you really have a servant's heart is to see what your reaction is when somebody treats you like one."
—Elizabeth Elliot

On July 4, 1881, at the age of twenty-five, Booker T. Washington became the first principal of the Tuskegee Institute (now Tuskegee University) in Alabama. For the next thirty-four years—until his death in 1915—Washington advocated for emancipated slaves and worked for higher education opportunities among African Americans. But his leadership didn't come without its challenges.

Shortly after stepping into his role at the Institute, Booker was walking by the home of a wealthy family. The lady of the house—not knowing who he was—came outside and asked Washington if he'd chop some wood for her. He rolled up his sleeves, chopped the wood, brought it into the house, and stacked the logs by the fireplace. Later, a young girl told the wealthy woman that Booker was the principal of the Tuskegee Institute.

> **Faithful service is all about doing, but faithful servants combine doing with being.**

Embarrassed by her request, the woman went to see Washington in his office the next morning. After she apologized profusely, Booker simply replied, "It's perfectly all right, Madam. Occasionally I enjoy a little manual labor. Besides, it's always a delight to do something for a friend." The woman shook his hand and left his office, but she didn't forget Washington's gracious response. Instead, she persuaded her friends to join her in generously donating thousands of dollars to the Tuskegee Institute.[107]

Booker T. Washington could have reminded this wealthy woman of his title. He could have leveraged his position to refuse her request. Instead, Booker picked up the towel and began to serve. He didn't just "do" servant acts; he exuded servant leadership. Faithful service is all about *doing*, but faithful servants combine *doing* with *being*. Jesus forms a faithful servant's heart, and their service is the outflow of His work inside them.

THE TWO SIDES OF SERVANT LEADERSHIP

There are two sides to servant leadership: *leading by serving* and *serving by leading*. What's the difference?

When you *lead by serving*, servanthood drives your leadership. You're not focused on the rights of leadership but on the responsibilities of leadership. Serving becomes your priority and your posture, and you look for meaningful ways to serve your team and set aside your preferences for the good of the organization. You don't just *act* like a servant. You *are a servant* by your character and the way you lead.

The other side of servant leadership—*serving by leading*—is also important. To serve by leading requires you to embrace your leadership gift. In other words, the best way you can serve the organization is to use your leadership gift to add the greatest value possible. Failure to lead—when you're called and gifted to do so—is poor stewardship. You serve by leading when you embrace your leadership ability, steward it wisely, use it humbly, and then grow it to its full capacity.

Leaders get in trouble when they swing to the extremes. If you *only* lead by serving, you're at risk of becoming nothing more than a "doer" or a "doormat." Rather than focusing on your highest priorities and setting clear boundaries, you become a *doer of tasks*. As a result, people take advantage of you and walk over you like a doormat.

At the other extreme, if you *only* serve by leading, you'll grow your leadership capacity but won't be willing to do anything "beneath" you. You'll lead without serving anyone in the process. You won't stoop down to help others step up. You'll have a *head* for leadership without a *heart* for people. You'll exercise competency without cultivating compassion.

Let me simplify this into two words: *priorities* and *pride*. When you *only* "lead by serving," your *priorities* get sidelined by distractions, menial tasks, and the demands of others. You spend most of your time working on everybody else's to-do list while ignoring the priorities where you can add the greatest value to your team and the organization. While you should serve others and offer to help, your job is not to do somebody else's job for them.

When you *only* "serve by leading," your *pride* poisons the heart of leadership. If you're not careful, your teams will begin to resent you because your ivory tower mentality keeps you isolated from the very people who are turning your vision into reality. Don't get so focused on leading the mission of the organization that you forget to serve the people in the organization.[108]

Both sides of the servant leader coin are essential. You must *lead by serving* and *serve by leading*. When you hold both sides in balance, you add the most value to the organization and the people.

HOW TO BE A SERVANT LEADER

The ultimate picture of a servant leader is Jesus. In two passages of Scripture (Matthew 20 and 23), Jesus gives us a mandate and a model of servant leadership to follow. In Matthew 20, Jesus corrects His disciples' misguided ambition to be the greatest in the Kingdom. And in Matthew 23, Jesus contrasts pharisaical leadership with servant leadership. From these two passages, we discover seven essential choices to become a servant leader.

1) Choose INTEGRITY over DUPLICITY

The Pharisees formed around 165 BC as a separatist group who wanted nothing to do with people who interpreted the Jewish law differently. The word *Pharisee* even means "to separate." And while they may have started with good intentions, the Pharisees eventually drifted down a deceptive path of pride.

These religious leaders became powerful during the four hundred years between the Old Testament and New Testament. During these "silent years," God didn't speak. So, the Pharisees made up for God's silence. They didn't just interpret the Law, but they *added* their own applications and regulations to the Law to ensure people didn't *break* the law.

> **When God stops speaking, don't put words in His mouth.**

By the time Jesus entered the picture, the Pharisees had a list of 613 laws. No wonder they didn't like Jesus. He reduced it down to two laws: love God and love people (see Matthew 22:37-40).

But here's the real problem.

The Pharisees began to view their man-made additions to the Law as having divine origin.[109] Again, this happened during the four hundred silent years between the Old and New Testaments. Therein lies an important lesson: when God stops speaking, don't put words in His mouth.

The Pharisees' man-made rules of righteousness became so dominant in their thinking that Jesus even told them, "You cancel the word of God for the sake of your own tradition" (Matthew 15:6). They defined their own standard of righteousness and then became experts at judging others based on that standard.[110]

But they didn't live it, and Jesus called them out on it.

One day, Jesus said to the crowds and His disciples:

"The teachers of religious law and the Pharisees are the official interpreters of the law of Moses. So practice and obey whatever they tell you, but don't follow their example. For they don't practice what they teach." —Matthew 23:2-3

These religious leaders were masters of duplicity. The knowledge in their heads never made it to their hearts. As a result, leadership became nothing more than a stage to act like somebody they weren't.

Proverbs 11:3 says, "The integrity of the upright guides them, but the unfaithful are destroyed by their duplicity" (NIV). A duplicitous leader is double-minded. They cannot serve others without thinking about how it will benefit themselves. But a servant leader is whole, complete, and undivided. They lead with integrity, setting an example that others can confidently follow. The apostle Peter said, "Don't lord it over the people assigned to your care, but lead them by your own good example" (1 Peter 5:3). Servant leaders don't dole out demands they're unwilling to model. They lead with integrity.

Do a careful search of your life for duplicitous behavior. Ask the Holy Spirit to reveal the areas where you've let integrity slip and invite Him to produce His fruit inside your heart. Being proactive about your integrity will help you catch lapses before they turn into sinkholes.

2) Choose PEOPLE over POWER

Jesus continued his description of the Pharisees when He said, "They crush people with unbearable religious demands and never lift a finger to ease the burden" (Matthew 23:4). These leaders enjoyed wielding power but not for the benefit of others. They used their man-made rules like whips to beat people into submission. Jesus, on the other hand, came to lighten your burden and give rest to your soul (Matthew 11:28-30).

The Pharisees weren't the only ones with power-hungry ambition. Jesus had to address the same cravings for power in His disciples too. When James and John began jockeying for the highest position in the Kingdom of God, Jesus called them together and said, "You've observed how godless rulers throw their weight around, how quickly a little power goes to their heads. It's not going to be that way with you" (Matthew 20:25-26, MSG). Jesus didn't play by the same rules. "Whoever wants to be great must become a servant. Whoever wants to be first among you must be your slave" (Matthew 20:26-27, MSG).

During the American Revolutionary War, George Washington rode up to a group of soldiers who did not recognize him. As these soldiers worked hard to raise a heavy beam into position, their corporal shouted his instructions to the men: "Now you have it! All ready! Pull!" As Washington observed the men, he asked the corporal why he wasn't helping the soldiers. Repulsed by his comment, the corporal replied, "Do you realize I am the corporal?"

> **We should put people over power by using our power to help people.**

Washington then dismounted his horse and joined the men in their work until the beam was securely in place. Before leaving, Washington turned to the corporal, wiped the perspiration from his face, and said, "If ever you need assistance like this again, call upon Washington, your commander-in-chief, and I will come."[111] Washington put the people before his power. He not only served by leading, but he led by serving.

Like Washington, serving *alongside* your team is one way to put people over power. Another strategy is to do what Max Dupree advised: "The leader is the servant who removes the obstacles that prevent people from doing their jobs."[112] In other words, we should put people over power by using our power to help people.

What can you do to remove obstacles for the teams you lead? Can you make systems more efficient? Can you remove unnecessary red tape? Can you empower people with power rather than crushing them with rules?

3) Choose SILENCE over SHOW

Michelangelo, the famed Italian painter, sculptor, and architect, had plenty to be proud of. But after the installation of the *Pieta*, Michelangelo had to look his pride in the eye and wrestle it to the ground. The *Pieta* is a sculpture of Jesus's dead body lying across the lap of His mother, Mary.

When the *Pieta* was put on display, Michelangelo overheard somebody attribute the sculpture to the work of another Italian sculptor, Cristoforo Solari. After hearing this remark, Michelangelo entered the chapel one night and chiseled onto the sash across Mary's chest, "Michelangelo Buonarroti, Florentine, was making this." Interestingly, the *Pieta* is the only work Michelangelo ever signed. He later regretted his outburst of pride and swore to never sign his work again.[113]

How often do we do good works for the glory of God, so long as our signature is prominently displayed? When we have influence, it's easy to attract attention to ourselves. After all, we think we have an image to uphold and a perception to project. That's what the Pharisees did. Jesus said, "Everything they do is for show. On their arms they wear extra wide prayer boxes with Scripture verses inside, and they wear robes with extra long tassels" (Matthew 23:5).

In obedience to Deuteronomy 6, the Pharisees wore religious prayer boxes that contained portions of the Scriptures. In addition, they wore robes with tassels along the hem. But because pride consumed them, they made these religious ornaments *extra* wide and *extra* long. The Pharisees basically said, "Look at me. Aren't I spiritual? Aren't I great?" The Message captures this verse with sobering conviction: "Their lives are perpetual fashion shows, embroidered prayer shawls one day and flowery prayers the next."

Jesus took a different approach: silence.

When He healed a man with leprosy, Jesus didn't turn the occasion into an opportunity for fanfare. Instead, He told the man not to tell anyone (see Luke 5:14). When He healed a deaf man, Jesus gave the same instructions to the crowd (Mark 7:36). Jesus wasn't looking for praise. He wasn't consumed with publicity or promotion but rather a mission to do His Father's will.

At its core, choosing silence over show is all about motives. It's an inside job. It's a matter of the heart. And that's what matters most to Jesus. Jesus sees right through our phony facades to the motives of the heart. In fact, on one occasion, after performing several miracles, people began placing their trust in Jesus. "But Jesus didn't trust them, because he knew all about people. No one needed to tell him about human nature, for he knew what was in each person's heart" (John 2:24-25). Yes, that's actually in the Bible. I'm guessing it's as convicting to you as it is for me.

The motive of a servant leader is to serve people for their good and God's glory. They don't turn every ministry moment into an opportunity to boost their social media following. They've learned the beauty of serving without having to let the world know about it.

Does this mean leaders should do everything in silence? I'm not sure that's even possible. But that's not my point. Instead, our motive for what we do must be grounded in serving rather than self-promotion. Let Jesus's words in Matthew 6:1-4 (MSG) drive this message deep into your soul:

> *"Be especially careful when you are trying to be good so that you don't make a performance out of it. It might be good theater, but the God who made you won't be applauding. When you do something for someone else, don't call attention to yourself. You've seen them in action, I'm sure—'playactors' I call them—treating prayer meeting and street corner alike as a stage, acting compassionate as long as someone is watching, playing to the crowds. They get applause, true, but that's all they get. When you help someone out, don't think about how it looks. Just do it—quietly and unobtrusively. That is the way your God, who conceived you in love, working behind the scenes, helps you out."*

Leaders who seek show over silence find themselves in a perpetual cycle of image management. Today's performance always needs to outdo yesterday's show. Not only is that unholy, it's also unsustainable and exhausting. Avoid that trap. Lead from a posture of silence, and let God worry about the show.

Where should you start? Do a genuine heart check. Why do you do what you do? What motives are driving your decisions, behaviors, and leadership? Instead of guessing, ask a trusted friend what they've observed in you.

4) Choose GIVING over GETTING

Several years ago, Karen and I visited Israel. We had never been to the Holy Land before, and we looked forward to following in the footsteps of Jesus through this ancient land. But halfway through our trip, everything changed.

COVID-19 suddenly shut down the world.

We quickly moved our departure up as people scrambled to get back home. When we arrived at Tel Aviv, we boarded our connecting flight to London. And when we landed at Heathrow Airport, everything felt chaotic. Flights were canceled, the airport overflowed with passengers, and we had to spend the night in London.

The next day, we headed to our gate, stood in a long line, and finally handed our tickets to the gate agent. She scanned the tickets, but nothing happened. I held my breath, thinking something must be wrong with the reservation. Then, to our total surprise, the computer spat out two different boarding passes. We'd been upgraded to business class.

Business class?

From London to Dallas/Fort Worth?

After doing cartwheels down the jet bridge, we boarded the plane and settled into our comfy seats. It was hard to look up at our fellow peasants as they walked back to coach to squeeze their butts into seventeen-inch seats.

But we managed.

And when our flight landed in DFW, and we all stood up to deplane, a man walked up behind me, looked at my business class seat, and said, "That looks really nice."

I smiled and said, "Yeah, we got upgraded."

I was smiling.

He wasn't.

We love perks, don't we? Especially when they're unexpected.

And so did the Pharisees. But they didn't treat perks like a pleasant surprise or an unsought blessing. They *expected* perks and privileges. They *expected* preferential treatment. After all, they were "spiritual."

Jesus said, "And they love to sit at the head table at banquets and in the seats of honor in the synagogues" (Matthew 23:6). In general, perks are not bad unless, of course, we adopt an attitude that says, *I deserve them, and I'm entitled to them.* That's when perks become problems. And that's why we need a filter to help us process them.

My friend Steve Moore created a great filter for perks when he developed these five thought-provoking questions:

- Do I need this—*fill in the blank*; bigger office, special parking space, or private bathroom—to do my job more effectively?
- Is this—*fill in the blank*—a legitimate reward for my performance?

- Does this—*fill in the blank*—create distance or separation, real or perceived, between me and the people I'm leading?
- Does this—*fill in the blank*—increase my vulnerability to pride and egocentrism?
- Would this—*fill in the blank*—make it hard for me to let go of my leadership role, even if I knew God was directing me to do so?[114]

I know, convicting, right? But the moment perks and privileges make us *feel* important is also the moment our identity has been hijacked by them. If *who* you are is based on *what* you have, then your life has become a hollow shell of deception.

Servant leaders *give* of their time, talent, treasure, and influence, but they don't give with strings attached. Why? Because *getting* isn't their goal. They steward resources to serve others. And on occasion, God will surprise them with unexpected blessings.

Serve to give, not to get. If God throws in an upgrade in the process, enjoy it. But don't flaunt it or slip into the subtle deception that you're better than anyone else. The five questions above will help you choose giving over getting, and they'll keep you centered when you're tempted to leverage leadership for personal gain.

5) Choose TOWELS over TITLES

The posture of Jesus's leadership is one of *towels* over *titles*. Before the Passover celebration, Jesus met with His disciples. John tells us, "So he got up from the table, took off his robe, wrapped a towel around his waist, and poured water into a basin. Then he began to wash the disciples' feet, drying them with the towel he had around him" (John 13:4-5). This was a humbling act, but the verse that precedes the act makes its significance even more profound.

Verse 3 says, "Jesus knew that the Father had given him authority over everything and that he had come from God and would return to God." Get the picture: the One with the *highest authority* assumed the lowest position. That's how Jesus led. He was a servant leader. He even washed the feet of the one who would betray him.

At that moment, none of us would have been on our knees washing dirty feet. If by chance we were—and if we knew about Judas's evil plot—we'd tuck a hammer in our belt to inflict pain on his big toe.

Not Jesus.

Towels took precedence over titles.

He concluded this humbling act by saying:

> *"I have given you an example to follow. Do as I have done to you. I tell you the truth, slaves are not greater than their master. Nor is the messenger more important than the one who sends the message. Now that you know these things, God will bless you for doing them." —John 13:15-17*

Jesus enjoyed the privileges of deity, but He set them aside to assume the position of a slave (see Philippians 2:7).

> **A title should be nothing more than a reminder that you get to serve more people.**

The Pharisees? Not so much.

Jesus described them like this:

> *"They love to receive respectful greetings as they walk in the marketplaces, and to be called 'Rabbi.'*
>
> *"Don't let anyone call you 'Rabbi,' for you have only one teacher, and all of you are equal as brothers and sisters. And don't address anyone here on earth as 'Father,' for only God in heaven is your Father. And don't let anyone call you 'Teacher,' for you have only one teacher, the Messiah."*
>
> —Matthew 23:7-10

The title "Rabbi" means "my great one," and the Pharisees considered it a coveted title.[115] In other words, titles—quite literally—defined greatness. These religious leaders savored their titles and shunned the towel.

Leadership author Gerald Brooks often says, "When you become a leader, you lose the right to think about yourself." There's nothing wrong with a title or position unless, of course, it makes you think you're better than everyone else. A title should be nothing more than a reminder that you get to serve more people. Where should you start?

- Avoid positional statements like, "I'm the boss" or "Because I said so."
- Move beyond positional leadership by building healthy relationships.
- Be compassionate and caring.
- Practice empathy.
- Ask, "How can I help?"
- Invest in the health and growth of your team.

- Make a list of meaningful ways to serve your team for their benefit, and then put your ideas into practice.

If you're going to choose towels over titles, you must get over yourself. If your identity is tied up in your title, you'll never be able to serve the people you lead.

6) Choose HUMILITY over HUBRIS

A few years ago, I preached a two-part series on the topic of pride. Two parts are about all anybody can handle, including me. After our second service that morning a man came up to me in the lobby and said, "I have a question to ask you. Can we meet privately for a moment?"

I said, "Sure," and we stepped inside the auditorium to talk.

Then, he delivered the sucker punch: "Are your sermons always so negative?"

I'll be honest, he caught me off guard. I had just preached a sermon on pride, and now this man blew a hole in *my* pride.

Hoping he didn't mean what he said, I asked, "Well, can you explain?"

He said, "Today, you talked about pride, and it just seemed really negative. I like to come to church and feel good. I like to hear something that will lift me up."

I said, "Well, pride is one of those topics that's kind of hard for all of us to hear. I'm not trying to be negative, but I *am* trying to challenge us with Jesus's words on the subject."

He kept digging.

"Do you *really* think anyone *here* struggles with pride?"

I wanted to say, "I've got a list," but I refrained.

"Well," I said, "after the first service some people asked me to pray with them because of their battle with pride."

Then, the real issue came to light.

"I just don't see it," he said. "I mean, *I* don't struggle with pride."

Houston, we have a problem.

Sound the alarm.

Warning! Warning!

Let me let you in on a little secret: if you can say *out loud* that you don't struggle with pride, you're guilty of pride. It's a struggle for me. It's a struggle for you. It's a struggle for all of us.

Years ago, I sat in my pastor's office for an annual review. His comments were glowing, and his tone was positive as he complimented my performance. But then he said one phrase that lodged in my mind: "You need to be a little more of a servant-leader."

Why did he say that?

Because my pride had undermined my ability to serve. Leading had become more important than serving. Something had to change, and it had to start with me climbing down from my pedestal and choosing the path of humility.

Author John Dickson framed it well when he said:

Humility is the noble choice to forgo your status, deploy your resources or use your influence for the good of others before yourself. . . . The humble person is marked by a willingness to hold power in service of others.[116]

Without humility, leaders become self-absorbed, self-promoting, and self-serving. Pride makes a god out of self.

This is where Jesus turns a corner in his teaching. After providing a detailed description of the Pharisees' misguided approach to leadership, Jesus said to his disciples, "The greatest among you must be a servant. But those who exalt themselves will be humbled, and those who humble themselves will be exalted" (Matthew 23:11-12). The Pharisees' hearts were cloaked in hubris, but Jesus called His followers to a posture of humility.

In this passage, we have a role to play, and God has a role to play. Our role is to humble ourselves, and when He sees fit, God's role is to exalt us. By "exalt," I don't mean worship (I'm just quoting Jesus). As long as we keep the roles in the right order, everything will turn out fine. But if we ever switch the roles, the outcome will be disastrous. In other words, if we exalt ourselves, then God will step into a different role—He'll humble us. I don't think that's the role any of us want God to play.

Pride is man's path to pursue favor; humility is God's path to give it to you. Pride is the exalted path that, in the end, is brought low; humility is the low path that, in the end, is exalted. Humble yourself, and let God handle the exalting as He sees best. Peter said, "So humble yourselves under the mighty power of God, and at the right time he will lift you up in honor" (1 Peter 5:6).

If you're having a hard time diagnosing whether pride has a grip on your life and leadership, then see if any of these faces of pride look familiar:

- Control: You have a need for power, titles, or authority.
- Capability: You brag about your accomplishments.
- Compensation: You feel entitled to perks and privileges.
- Character: You're reckless in your attitude toward sin.
- Conversations: You talk more than you listen.
- Correction: You respond defensively to correction.
- Capacity: You have an exaggerated view of your talent.
- Competence: You pride yourself on being in the know.

- Comparison: You draw your identity from being better than others.
- Credit: You don't like to share the credit or limelight with others.
- Compliments: You're hesitant to affirm or compliment others.
- Confidence: Your faith and reliance are in yourself rather than God.

I know, another convicting list. Some of them are especially hard to write. What about you? Which "face of pride" do you struggle with the most? If you really want to know the answer, share this list with a friend, family member, coworker, or boss and ask for their perspective. Then, take some time to humble yourself before the Lord and lay your ego at His feet.

Author and theologian John Stott once said:

The authority by which the Christian leader leads is not power but love, not force but example, not coercion but reasoned persuasion. Leaders have power, but power is safe only in the hands of those who humble themselves to serve.[117]

To be entrusted with power is a great responsibility. Servant leaders steward that responsibility out of a spirit of humility.

7) Choose SACRIFICE over SECURITY

Jesus is the ultimate model of sacrifice over security. In Matthew 20:28, He said, "For even the Son of Man came not to be served but to serve others and to give his life as a ransom for many." Jesus expected to make sacrifices and did so all the way to His death at the cross.

It is rumored that American missionary Adoniram Judson once said, "There is no success without sacrifice. If you succeed without sacrifice it is because someone has suffered before you. If you sacrifice without success it is because someone will succeed after."[118] That's a great perspective on sacrifice.

When you make sacrifices, you give up something you love for something you love even more—something for the good of others or for eternal value. Crises don't pay attention to schedules, so there's no doubt you'll sacrifice time. Leadership is a magnet for pain, so you'll sacrifice ease and comfort. And leadership is no popularity contest, so you'll sacrifice people-pleasing. If you're not willing to make sacrifices, you shouldn't lead. Sacrifice comes with the territory.

> **In leadership, you can pay a sacrificial price now or an ominous price later.**

Servant leaders are prepared to make these sacrifices, but they're also careful not to sacrifice their faith, their values, or their family. They set boundaries to protect their highest priorities, while at the same time choosing *sacrifice* over *security*.

Jesus concluded his description of the Pharisees with several sobering statements that begin with these words: "What sorrow awaits you teachers of religious law and you Pharisees. Hypocrites!" (Matthew 23:13). Jesus makes it clear: the Pharisees' approach to life and leadership would eventually catch up with them. In leadership, you can pay a sacrificial price now or an ominous price later. Either way, there is a price to pay—now or for eternity. Rather than leveraging leadership for personal gain, make sacrifices today to serve the greater good.

When we courageously and consistently make these seven choices, we model servant leadership. To help you put them into action, check out Leadership Tool #9: 7 Servant-Leader Choices. And if you're wondering whether you're already a servant leader, then let the words of Elizabeth Elliot be your litmus test: "The best way to find out whether you really have a servant's heart is to see what your reaction is when somebody treats you like one."[119]

INSANELY PRACTICAL REFLECTION AND DISCUSSION

1. What stands out to you the most about the difference between Jesus's leadership and the leadership of the Pharisees?
2. Humility is an underlying theme in Jesus's emphasis on servant leadership. What would it look like to walk in a spirit of humility in the areas where you lead and among the teams where you serve?
3. Which of the seven servant leadership choices speaks to you the most? Why?
4. What are some practical tips you gleaned from this chapter that would help you be a servant leader at work, with your family, in the church, and in your community?

LEADERSHIP TOOL #9
7 Servant-Leader Choices

Jesus taught and modeled servant leadership by emphasizing seven important choices. In the chart below, answer each question in the space provided to help you evaluate your behavior and make the right servant-leader choice.

7 SERVANT-LEADER CHOICES
Choose INTEGRITY over DUPLICITY: In what areas of my life do I lack integrity, and how do I need to begin practicing what I preach?
Choose PEOPLE over POWER: In what ways can I use my power to serve people, remove obstacles for people, eliminate red tape, and empower others?
Choose SILENCE over SHOW: How do my motives in leadership need to change, and how can I deflect attention from myself to others?
Choose GIVING over GETTING: What are my expectations toward perks and privileges, and how does my attitude need to align with Jesus's example?
Choose TOWELS over TITLES: How do I need to stop drawing attention to my title and position, and what are three ways I can serve my team?

Choose HUMILITY over HUBRIS: Which "Faces of Pride" do I struggle with most, and what steps will I take to humble myself in these areas?
Choose SACRIFICE over SECURITY: What do I need to begin sacrificing in my leadership: people-pleasing, time, comfort, money, or something else?

Download the 7 Servant-Leader Choices tool at insanelypracticalleadership.com.

CHAPTER 10

HOW TO COMMUNICATE WITH PEOPLE

"Words kill, words give life; they're either poison or fruit—you choose."
—**Proverbs 18:21 (MSG)**

It was January 28, 1986, and I was running an errand with a friend for our high school journalism class. As we drove down Altamesa Boulevard in Fort Worth, we suddenly heard the news on the radio: the space shuttle *Challenger* had just exploded.

Seventeen months earlier, on August 27, 1984, President Ronald Reagan had announced a teacher would be the first private citizen to join the crew of the space shuttle. More than ten thousand teachers applied, but Christa McAuliffe, a middle school teacher from Concord, New Hampshire, was chosen for this historic mission.

After multiple delayed attempts to launch the *Challenger*, seven crew members finally boarded the spacecraft for this monumental moment. But seventy-three seconds after lifting off from Cape

Canaveral, the six-day mission abruptly ended when the *Challenger* exploded above the Atlantic Ocean.[120]

The catastrophic event stunned the nation. That evening, President Reagan was scheduled to deliver his annual State of the Union Address. Instead, he addressed a mourning nation from the Oval Office. He hailed the *Challenger* Seven as heroes, shared words of courage and hope, and tried to comfort school children across the nation who had witnessed the tragedy from televisions in their classrooms.

President Reagan went on to establish a commission chaired by former Secretary of State William P. Rogers. What came to be known as the Rogers Commission Report identified the cause of the explosion: an O-ring seal had failed.

But it turns out, the failure was much deeper.

In addition to an equipment failure, The Rogers Commission Report revealed an organizational failure: "systemic organizational and cultural elements . . . led to the decision to launch *Challenger* on that day."[121]

What exactly were those "systemic organizational and cultural elements?" Three of them were directly related to poor communication:

> *One problem was a lack of effective communication between the decision-makers—non-technical people—and the technicians and engineers who were painfully aware of operational problems as the Challenger project progressed. The second problem addressed by the Commission was the lack of a formal communication channel which resulted in "management isolation." The third problem was attributed to "selective listening."*[122]

The night before the launch, Bob Ebeling and four other engineers from Morton Thiokol raised concerns about the forecast temperatures and the impact they could have on the O-rings. Alarmed over the risk, Ebeling and the other Thiokol engineers recommended the launch be grounded if the temperature fell below fifty-three degrees. But senior management overruled the recommendation.

That night, Bob Ebeling told his wife, Darlene, "It's going to blow up."

And the next day, it did.

Ebeling and his engineering colleagues sat in a conference room at Thiokol's headquarters in Utah. As they watched a giant television screen, their hearts broke as the shuttle exploded before their eyes. Immediately, they knew the cause of the disaster.

In an interview thirty years later, Ebeling said, "I was one of the few that was really close to the situation. Had they listened to me and wait[ed] for a weather change, it might have been a completely different outcome."[123]

The Rogers Commission Report stated:

> *"Failures in communication" resulted in the decision to launch "based on incomplete and sometimes misleading information, a conflict between engineering data and management judgments, and a NASA management structure that permitted internal flight safety problems to bypass key Shuttle managers."*[124]

Despite the efforts of Ebeling and the other engineers, "selective listening" on the part of senior management won the day. NASA went forward with the flight, and disaster ensued. Seven innocent lives were lost.

In most cases, poor communication isn't a matter of life and death. And yet, it is. King Solomon said, "Words kill, words give life; they're either poison or fruit—you choose" (Proverbs 18:21, MSG).

FOUR TYPES OF COMMUNICATION

Communication is so simple until it's not. Getting what's in my head into your head seems like a straight line until the twists and turns of assumptions, tone, and confusion sabotage the mission. What seems so clear to me is a perplexing maze to you.

Author and leadership expert Michael Hyatt has tried to demystify the maze by identifying four types of communication: no communication, garbled communication, implied communication, and clear communication. These communication types are characterized by vagueness or specificity and unexpressed or expressed.

- *No Communication* is vague and unexpressed, resulting in ignorance.
- *Garbled Communication* is expressed but vague, resulting in confusion.
- *Implied Communication* is specific but unexpressed, resulting in frustration.
- *Clear Communication* is specific and expressed, resulting in understanding.[125]

Hyatt goes on to observe, "Most under-communication is inadvertent. People are simply unaware of the gap between what's in their mind and what's in yours, and you suffer from the same lack of awareness."[126]

How do we deal with these all-too-common communication failures? What does it take to move from garbled or implied communication to clear communication? It starts with the right skills and a good system.

HOW TO COMMUNICATE WITH OTHERS

One study found that 66 percent of business leaders experience miscommunication at least once a day and 48 percent multiple times a day.[127] Communication is a critical leadership skill, and without it, you won't effectively connect with others. So, what are the skills of good communication? Start with these six.

1) Life-Giving Content

Each Valentine's Day, Karen and I go on a date and enjoy a nice meal together. During one of these special evenings, Karen said, "Let's go back and forth and share one thing we love about each other." Karen began, "I love how kind you are." I smiled and replied, "I love your laugh. . . . It always warms my heart to hear you laugh." Back and forth we shared. We affirmed one another's qualities—physical, relational, intellectual, emotional, and spiritual. It was a beautiful evening marked by an abundance of life-giving words.

Speaking life-giving words is more than a great idea for a date night; they're a great way to approach any human connection. Proverbs 10:11 says, "The words of the godly are a life-giving fountain; the words of the wicked conceal violent intentions." If the content of your communication is lifeless, degrading, or untrue, you'll never connect with people. The substance of your words must pass three tests to be life-giving content.

First, are your words *truthful?* The apostle Paul said, "Instead, we will speak the truth in love, growing in every way more and more like Christ, who is the head of his body, the church" (Ephesians 4:15). I'll address the "in love" part at another point, so let's begin with the truth. When you speak to your coworkers, is your speech truthful and trustworthy, or do you fabricate your stories, exaggerate the numbers, and invent tall tales to make yourself look good? In the words of Buddy the Elf to the "fake" Santa Claus at Gimbels department store, do you "sit on a throne of lies"?[128]

Second, are your words *wise?* What separates a truthful word from a wise word? Truthful words are facts, but wise words are discerning and full of perspective. You don't need to be a sage to offer words of wisdom. Instead, lean on Scripture, experience, and personal reflection to speak wise words. The outcome will be worth it. As King Solomon said, "Some people make cutting remarks, but the words of the wise bring healing" (Proverbs 12:18). Your wise words can be a source of healing.

Third, are your words *helpful?* If somebody helps you organize your garage, complete a project at work, or prepare a big meal on Thanksgiving Day, their actions are a gift to you. The same is true with words. Paul said, "Watch the way you talk. Let nothing foul or dirty come out of your mouth. Say only what helps, each word a gift" (Ephesians 4:29, MSG). When people speak helpful words to us, they're a gift of encouragement, hope, and inspiration. And when we speak helpful words, we give strength to the people we love, lead, and serve. King Solomon said, "The lips of the godly speak helpful words, but the mouth of the wicked speaks perverse words" (Proverbs 10:32).

Karen is a licensed professional counselor, and she regularly shares practical tips to help people navigate difficult situations. One tip she offers is to say this simple phrase to people who speak hurtful or disparaging words to you: "That's not helpful." Those three words pack a punch. They're direct but kind. They're candid but caring. They let people know their words have just crossed a boundary.

What about you? Are your words life-giving? This doesn't mean every conversation is easy. As a leader, you'll have plenty of tough conversations to address difficult issues, but at the end of the day, your words in every conversation should be truthful, wise, and helpful.

2) Clear Speech

Mark Twain once said, "The difference between the right word and the almost right word is the difference between lightning and the lightning bug."[129] If people can't understand what you're saying, everything you say undermines your credibility.

There are three parts to clear speech. The first aspect is obvious: *clarity*. When your clarity decreases, everyone else's blood pressure increases. Lack of clarity creates frustration while simultaneously immobilizing team members' ability to act. Clear communication, on the other hand, creates understanding, confidence, and movement. At NASA, confusion between decision-makers and engineers led to the failed interpretation of data regarding the O-rings.[130] That lack of clarity resulted in disaster.

The second aspect of clear speech is *conciseness*. When we ramble on and on about a topic, it becomes an emotional drain on our hearers. Before long, they stop listening and start wondering when we'll shut up. Keep in mind the wisdom of Proverbs 17:27-28: "A truly wise person uses few words; a person with understanding is even-tempered. Even fools are thought wise when they keep silent; with their mouths shut, they seem intelligent." The more you talk, the less people are impressed.

The final part of clear speech is *pace*. The average pace for a conversation is 150 words per minute.[131] If your pace is too quick, people won't follow what you have to say, and if it's too slow, people will disengage. The proper pace creates a communication rhythm that makes it easy to follow. It helps people connect and engage without being confused by a rapid pace or bored by a slow pace. Clarity, conciseness, and pace ensure our communication is clear, engaging, and easy to follow.

3) Positive Tone

Eeyore is the donkey in the fictional story of Winnie-the-Pooh. No matter the situation, Eeyore's tone is always negative. He'd say, "Could be worse. Not sure how, but it could be." And his attempts to be positive were always draped in a depressive tone: "It's snowing still. And freezing. However, we haven't had an earthquake lately." Eeyore's name has become synonymous with a negative tone and a pessimistic outlook.[132]

Tone is the attitude behind the words you speak. You can communicate in a positive tone or a negative tone, an open tone or a defensive tone, a hopeful tone or a depressive tone. As the leader, you set the overall tone and temperature for the team.

Tone also has a direct bearing on our productivity at work. According to a study by The Harris Poll on behalf of Grammarly Business, when the tone of communication is positive, knowledge workers are more likely to respond more quickly, do work at a higher quality, be more responsive to future requests, and perceive the sender more positively.[133]

As I noted earlier, we must speak the truth, but Paul instructs us to do so "in love" (Ephesians 4:15). Truth without love turns words into weapons. King Solomon offers some good tone-setting wisdom in Proverbs 15:1: "A gentle answer deflects anger, but harsh words make tempers flare." Gentleness cultivates a non-defensive posture in communication and invites others into the conversation. Whatever you do, avoid an "Eeyore tone" and learn to speak with positivity and grace.

4) Curious Questions

One of the greatest compliments I've ever received is, "Stephen, you ask great questions." I've heard that comment while *receiving* coaching and *giving* coaching. It's an imperative ingredient to unearthing new insights into some of my favorite topics—such as leadership, personal growth, and organizational development. But it's also essential to healthy interpersonal communication.

Asking thoughtful questions invites others into the conversation. Without questions, you're simply dispersing information. Author Mark Miller observed, "Asking questions is not a sign of weakness—it is a sign of wisdom."[134] In short, good questions ensure you're connecting with the other person, inviting feedback, and building a bridge to active listening.

Questions are emboldened when combined with curiosity. "I have no special talents," Albert Einstein once said. "I am only passionately curious."[135] Such curiosity leads to follow-up questions that deepen conversations and strengthen understanding. You don't just want to hear what others say; you want to understand the heart of the matter. Curiosity digs beneath the surface and helps you shift from being interesting to being interested.

5) Active Listening

I was once in a meeting with a consultant who was coaching a group of pastors from a wide variety of backgrounds and life experiences. These were sharp leaders who desired to make a meaningful contribution, and they had gathered to learn from this expert guide. But one of the pastors in attendance dominated the conversation, and the longer I sat in the meeting, the more I made an observation: the one who talked the most had the least to say. In fact, the more he spoke, the less credible he became.

It's easy to assume we're good listeners, especially when we're gifted in other areas of leadership. But as author Robert K. Greenleaf observed, "Don't assume, because you are intelligent, able, and well-motivated, that you are open to communication, that you know how to listen."[136] Leading and listening are two different skills, but leading *without* listening will significantly handicap your leadership.

Attention span is one factor that affects good listening. Unfortunately, our attention span has declined over the years, now sitting at a shocking 8.25 seconds—shorter than a goldfish.[137] And cell phones don't help. We're addicted to small hits of dopamine every time we check our phones—144 times per day.[138] We forget that our attention is the precious currency we pay to show people how much we care. Without your undivided attention, you communicate an entirely different message: *You're not important, and what you have to say doesn't matter.*

Active listening helps you fully engage in the conversation. Rather than listening "cafeteria style"—listening to a little bit of *this* but not a whole lotta *that*—active listeners are interested without interrupting. As James wisely noted, "You must all be quick to listen, slow to speak, and slow to get angry" (James 1:19). Interruption is disrespectful and is often driven by false assumptions. But when we patiently listen, we create space for understanding to mature.

Another important part of active listening is body language. Psychologist Albert Mehrabian's research on body language reveals that "the total impact of a message is about 7 percent verbal (words only) and 38 percent vocal (including tone of voice, inflection, and other sounds) and 55 percent nonverbal."[139] It's not just what *you* say and what *they* say that matters; it's also the unspoken communication of your eyes, face, and posture. Does your body language (and theirs) say, *I'm engaged* or *I'm bored*? Do you lean in with curiosity, or are you distracted by what's happening around you? As Peter Drucker once said, "The most important thing in communication is to hear what isn't being said."[140]

6) Controlled Response

Several years ago, Karen and I visited Hoover Dam. When I first walked onto the Dam, I was awe-struck by the enormity of the structure. At its base, Hoover Dam is 660 feet thick, taming the Colorado River along the Nevada-Arizona border. This marvel of human ingenuity does more than hold back flood waters. It also irrigates two million acres, generates hydroelectric power for 1.3 million people, and provides municipal water to cities like Los Angeles, Phoenix, and Tucson.[141]

To put the power of the Hoover Dam into perspective, consider what would happen if an earthquake crippled the dam. Not only would the water supply for twenty-five million people be impacted,[142] but Lake Mead would release enough water to cover ten million acres one foot deep. That's larger than the entire state of New Jersey.[143]

Whether it's spinning turbines to generate power or flooding cities and creating widespread destruction, the water holds tremendous power. The difference between one scenario and the other is *control*. When everything is functioning properly, the water represents *power under control*. But in the case of an earthquake, it releases a crushing flood of *uncontrolled power*.

Our response to others in day-to-day conversations acts much the same way. When our response is controlled, it's a source of life. When uncontrolled, our response unleashes a torrent of devastation. That's why it's wise to heed the apostle Paul's instructions: "Always be humble and gentle" (Ephesians 4:2). Being a gentle leader might sound weak and wimpy, but the word "gentle" actually means *power under control*. A gentle response isn't dependent on having power, but it does reveal whether or not power has you.

Communication follows a predictable cycle: you speak, they speak, and then you respond. Your response dictates the ultimate outcome. It either validates or villainizes the other person. It communicates how much you care or how little you value them. When your response exhibits "power under control," it removes fear and allows the relationship to breathe. So, what does a controlled response look like? It shows four qualities: restraint, clarification, grace, and timing.

First, an effective response always shows *restraint*. Concentration camp survivor Viktor Frankl once said, "Between stimulus and response there is a space. In that space is our power to choose a response. In our response lies our growth and our freedom."[144] The stimulus Frankl endured in the camps was brutal and horrific, and yet he still controlled his response to the pain he endured and the people who tortured him. How much more should we be able to control our response to the words people speak to us? Restraint is the governor of your response. Blowing up or lashing out will only sabotage your efforts to communicate and connect.

Second, a controlled response seeks *clarification*. Author and business professional Cheryl Bachelder observed this:

When leaders get mad, listening and learning go out the window. Mad leaders know exactly what they want to say. They cut to the chase and tell you exactly how they feel—which is highly efficient but very ineffective. The unfortunate truth: efficiency with people ruins relationships.[145]

When we lean in to listen and learn, we discover the clarification that keeps us from jumping to conclusions. King Solomon warned, "Spouting off before listening to the facts is both shameful and foolish" (Proverbs 18:13). To seek clarification, begin by asking questions, listen carefully, and then state what you're hearing back to the person speaking to you. This will increase understanding, decrease ambiguity, and eliminate vague and elusive feelings that often fuel uncontrolled responses.

Third, a controlled response is *gracious*. The heart behind your words is as important as the words themselves. The apostle Paul said, "Let your conversation be gracious and attractive so that you will have the right response for everyone" (Colossians 4:6). A gracious response puts the person before your opinions. It's kind, courteous, and empathetic. These qualities require focus and intentionality. As author Mark Miller said, "Empathy is a skill powered by energy. No energy, no empathy."[146] How much energy are you putting into a gracious and empathetic response?

Finally, a controlled response is sensitive to *timing*. Our words get us into trouble when our timing is off. For example, telling your spouse, "I have something really important to talk about," when they're walking out the door to make a major presentation at work is bad timing. Your comment will be a woodpecker chipping away at their mind when they need to be fully engaged in this make-or-break presentation. Or walking into your boss's office to ask for a raise when the company's stock just plummeted is bad timing and tone deaf. Proverbs 15:23 offers a better strategy: "Everyone enjoys a fitting reply; it is wonderful to say the right thing at the right time!"

When you communicate with these six skills, you'll effectively and consistently connect with people. Consider the alternative:

- Without *Life-Giving Content*, your words are hurtful and degrading.
- Without *Clear Speech*, your communication is confusing.
- Without *Positive Tone*, your dialogue is negative and defensive.
- Without *Curious Questions*, your conversations remain shallow.
- Without *Active Listening*, you appear distracted and disinterested.

- Without *Controlled Response*, your overreaction damages the relationship.

Each key plays an important role in communication. Together, they deepen rich conversation and compound relational connection.

Your communication may not be a matter of life and death like the space shuttle *Challenger*, but it's certainly a matter of health vs. dysfunction. Good communication fosters good relationships and contributes to a healthy organizational culture. The six communication *skills* set the starting pace, but you also need a good communication *system*.

TEAM: A COMMUNICATION SYSTEM

Maintaining healthy and consistent communication throughout an organization requires a clear process. I recommend a simple four-part system: TEAM—Tools, Education, Accountability, and Meetings.

Tools

Start by identifying the tools your organization will use to facilitate effective and efficient communication. These tools may include software, apps, email, texting, and any number of technological solutions. The size of the organization will obviously determine which solutions make the most sense.

Education

Next, train team members *how* to communicate. Begin by educating your team on the six communication skills: life-giving content, clear speech, positive tone, curious questions, active listening, and controlled response. These skills significantly impact the health and culture of the organization, and they'll mitigate conflict and lapses in communication.

Accountability

By accountability, I'm not talking about an overbearing, fear-inducing system that puts everyone on edge. Instead, if communication breaks down, you, as the leader, are responsible and accountable for identifying what's wrong and then developing a plan to fix it. Without accountability, communication gaps arise and multiply.

Meetings

Meetings are one of the best places to facilitate good communication. However, this is only true if the meetings are characterized by the following four traits:

- *Well-Organized.* Meetings must happen at the right time, in the right place, and with the right people.
- *Well-Planned.* Meetings must follow a purposeful agenda that delivers the intended results.
- *Well-Led.* A designated leader should respectfully facilitate meetings with a positive tone and a well-paced agenda that starts and ends on time.
- *Well-Ended.* Meetings must end with clear next steps that define who will do what and by when.

When meetings are characterized by these traits, communication becomes clear and consistent.

William H. Whyte once said, "The great enemy of communication is the illusion of it."[147] In the case of the *Challenger*, that illusion led to the loss of seven lives. To strengthen team relationships and foster a healthy culture, leaders and team members must employ the six communication skills and activate the TEAM communication system. This is the roadmap to effective communication. To help you get started, use Leadership Tool #10: Communication Rater.

INSANELY PRACTICAL REFLECTION AND DISCUSSION

1. How do the words of Proverbs 18:21 (MSG) challenge you: "Words kill, words give life; they're either poison or fruit—you choose"?
2. Which of the six communication skills would make the biggest difference right now among the teams you're serving alongside (life-giving content, clear speech, positive tone, curious questions, active listening, or controlled response)?
3. What does it look like to speak in a positive tone when you're having tough conversations?
4. What practical steps could you take to implement the TEAM Communication System in your context at work (Tools, Education, Accountability, Meetings)?

LEADERSHIP TOOL #10
Communication Rater

The challenge with communication is that we don't hear how we come across to others. To help you improve, give the evaluation form below to a boss, a coworker, or your entire team and ask them to rate how you speak, listen, and respond.

NAME OF PERSON BEING EVALUATED:			
I want to improve my interpersonal communication, and I value your feedback. Using the Green/Yellow/Red rating system, please rate me in the six skills below to help me understand how I speak, listen, and respond to you in conversations. Green means I practice this skill with proficiency. Yellow means I need to make some improvements in this skill. Red means I'm weak in this skill. In addition, feel free to offer additional observations below along with any tips to improve my communication.			
COMMUNICATION POSTURE & SKILLS	RATING		
	Green	Yellow	Red
SKILL #1: LIFE-GIVING CONTENT			
Truthful: You speak the truth and are fully trustworthy.			
Wise: You speak wise words that offer valuable perspective.			
Helpful: Your words are genuinely helpful to me.			
SKILL #2: CLEAR SPEECH			
Clarity: You speak in a clear and easy-to-understand way.			
Conciseness: You speak concisely and don't ramble on.			
Pace: You speak at a pace that's easy to follow.			

SKILL #3: POSITIVE TONE			
Optimism: An optimistic outlook comes through your words.			
Tone: Your tone is positive and encouraging.			
SKILL #4: CURIOUS QUESTIONS			
Curiosity: You show curiosity about what I have to say.			
Questions: You ask good questions and cultivate dialogue.			
SKILL #5: ACTIVE LISTENING			
Attentiveness: You listen carefully when I'm speaking.			
Interested: You show genuine interest in what I have to say.			
Body Language: Your body language is engaged.			
SKILL #6: CONTROLLED RESPONSE			
Restraint: You show self-restraint and don't interrupt.			
Clarification: You seek clarification if you don't understand.			
Gracious: You are kind and empathetic in your responses.			
Timing: Your responses to me are well-timed.			
YOUR OBSERVATIONS OR TIPS TO IMPROVE MY COMMUNICATION			

Download the Communication Rater at insanelypracticalleadership.com.

CHAPTER 11

HOW TO LEAD THROUGH CONFLICT

"The way in which you handle conflict provides an unfiltered picture of your spiritual, emotional, and relational maturity."
—Stephen Blandino

From an early age, Frank Worsley found himself captivated by the open seas. He was once asked to transport a horse to the end of the harbor in Akaroa, New Zealand, but Frank's adventurous spirit was too rambunctious to walk back home after making the delivery.[148] Instead, he and his brother built a raft from harakeke reeds to make the journey home across the harbor. They tied a couple of sticks together to make a mast and yard, turned their jackets into sails, and then carved paddles from planks to navigate the choppy waters.[149] That same thrill-seeking spirit primed his steadfast decision at the age of fifteen to pursue life on the ocean.

After acquiring twenty-seven years of experience at sea, Frank had a dream one night of sailing a ship past icebergs down Burlington Street in London. The next day, as he walked down that very street, he noticed a sign advertising an upcoming Imperial Trans-Antarctic Expedition. Worsley went inside for an interview, and Sir Ernest Shackleton hired him to be the captain of the ship *Endurance*.[150]

I recounted Shackleton's astonishing Antarctic journey in chapter 8, but what I didn't tell you was how critical Captain Frank Worsley was to the expedition. Worsley had the arduous task of navigating the floes and icebergs that eventually brought the *Endurance* to a halt, permanently trapped, and eventually crushed by the ice and swallowed by the sea. But the need for Worsley's experience wouldn't end with the sinking of *Endurance*. Quite the opposite. It would save the crew's lives.

NAVIGATIONAL GENIUS

On April 9, 1916, when Shackleton gave the order to launch the lifeboats, the crew was hounded by a merciless ocean and threatened by whales, icebergs, and gale-force winds. In the clutch of these cruel conditions, Captain Worsley had to guide the boats. With rare glimpses of the sun, he made valiant attempts to navigate the men toward land. Worsley didn't sleep for eighty hours, and finally, after a heroic effort, they reached Elephant Island on April 15. It was the first time in 497 days that they stood on solid ground.[151]

Shackleton congratulated Worsley on his extraordinary seafaring skills, but his navigational genius didn't end there. When the Boss assembled a crew for the journey to South Georgia, Captain Worsley would play a most critical role. South Georgia was only twenty-five miles at its widest point, and 850 miles away. Finding this needle in the haystack of a vast ocean without Worsley's navigation skills would be near impossible.[152] Worsley gathered his sextant and navigational tables and charts. In addition, he brought another sextant which belonged to Hubert Hudson, as well as the only chronometer that remained among the group.[153]

By April 26, they entered the Drake Passage, 128 miles from Elephant Island. The crew experienced gale-force winds and fifty-foot waves known as "Cape Horn Rollers."[154] Despite the severity of the winds and the enormity of the waves, Captain Worsley did his best to steer through the furious ocean. His navigational books were soaked with ocean water. Losing them would be disastrous. "The Nautical Almanac, with its tables of sun and star positions, was in even worse shape.... its pages had to be carefully peeled apart to separate them."[155] But Worsley's skills were their only hope for reaching South Georgia. After three barbaric days, he finally caught a glimpse of the sun. He pulled out his sextant to get a sight, and then yelled, "Mark!" Shackleton recorded the time, and then Worsley did his calculations to determine how much progress they had made.[156]

In the span of sixteen days, Captain Worsley got only four shadowy sightings of the sun. Despite these sparse glimmers of hope, his ability for dead reckoning gave him the instinct to know his position, even without the help of navigational aids.[157]

The captain's course-plotting knack paid off.

They sighted land.

Mountains arose out of the ocean and soared over the horizon. "We've done it," Shackleton shouted.

After two more days of struggle, they reached the island on May 10, 1916. It had been 522 days since they originally left South Georgia. But with the ocean behind them and mountains in front of them, once again, Captain Worsley would have to guide their treacherous journey for more than twenty-five miles, scaling mountains some 10,000 feet high.[158] Because of his extraordinary skill, they reached the Stromness whaling station where the men found safety, and in the next four months, they were able to rescue the remaining men stranded on Elephant Island.

NAVIGATING STORMY SEAS

Nothing compares to the stormy seas Sir Ernest Shackleton, Captain Frank Worsley, and their courageous crew navigated during this twenty-two-month nightmare. The journey from Elephant Island to South Georgia is considered one of the most heroic ocean voyages of all time, and Worsley's navigation skills were indispensable to their success.[159] Consider these realities:

- Rare glimpses of the sun created long gaps between the times when Worsley could take readings with his sextant.
- The violent waves made it difficult to bring the sun down onto the horizon so Worsley could capture accurate readings.
- Worsley was forced to rely on gut instinct and dead reckoning to estimate their exact location on the open seas.
- Worsley had to navigate around and through constant threats, such as floes, icebergs, whales, giant waves, strong currents, and gale-force winds.
- The physical, mental, and emotional conditions were unbearable, including weeks of darkness, frostbitten fingers,

salt-water boils, constant cold, diarrhea, seasickness, and the lack of food and fresh water.

And yet—despite all these hardships, diversions, and far-from-optimal conditions—Frank Worsley successfully navigated the most brutal and unpredictable waters on earth—the Weddell Sea and the Drake Passage.

HOW TO LEAD THROUGH CONFLICT

Why are we revisiting the story of *Endurance* and Captain Worsley's extraordinary navigational skills? Because they powerfully resemble the navigational challenges you'll face when you lead through *conflict*.

Conflict is unpredictable.
Conflict is unstable.
Conflict is unavoidable.

> **How you deal with conflict reveals the level of your maturity.**

Like the giant waves and hurricane-force winds the crew of the *Endurance* encountered, conflict is full of unseen forces that catch you by surprise and unknown dynamics that undermine your best efforts.

When you're navigating conflict, it's difficult to accurately read what the parties in the conflict think, want, or expect.

Furthermore, all kinds of variables are at play in conflict resolution. Opposition looms large like a giant iceberg, and unseen motives act like the undercurrent of an ocean, quickly changing the course of your direction. One wrong word, one mishap, and one lapse in judgment can sink your efforts to resolve conflict and find a way forward.

Many good-hearted pastors have crashed because they didn't know how to resolve conflict. Many executives with bold visions and audacious plans have been crushed when the ice floes of resistance stopped them dead in their tracks. If you can't navigate conflict, you won't be a successful leader. That sounds blunt—perhaps even unreasonable—but it's true. Conflict is inevitable in leadership, and your ability to steer through it will determine how far you go.

Here's another sobering truth: how you deal with conflict reveals the level of your maturity.

Let that sink in.

The way in which you handle conflict provides an unfiltered picture of your spiritual, emotional, and relational maturity.

So, where do you begin? How do you successfully lead through conflict with so many changing dynamics and unpredictable challenges? Effective conflict resolution requires six ingredients—with the core characteristic being your ability to cultivate trust.

1) Cultivate Trust

Trust doesn't just play *a* role in conflict resolution; it plays the *central role*. The most difficult conflicts to traverse are the ones where trust has been broken. Thus, trust is the *starting place* and the *driving force* behind effective conflict resolution. Cultivating trust doesn't happen by accident. It requires a well-designed P.L.A.N.:

Posture. Trust begins when we approach people and conflict with the right posture. Some leaders take the posture of a *pretender.* They pretend the conflict doesn't exist, turning a blind eye to what's really happening. Others take the posture of a *historian.* This person keeps a record of wrongs so they can remind the other person of all their mistakes. Then, there's the *judge*. This posture turns conflict into a court date so you can find the person guilty.

None of these postures—the pretender, historian, or judge—will resolve conflict. Instead, Jesus calls us to assume the posture of a *restorer*. He said:

> *This is how I want you to conduct yourself in these matters. If you enter your place of worship and, about to make an offering, you suddenly remember a grudge a friend has against you, abandon your offering, leave immediately, go to this friend and make things right. Then, and only then, come back and work things out with God. —Matthew 5:23-24 (MSG, emphasis added)*

Jesus doesn't permit us to stew with anger or blast people on social media. Instead, He tells us to address conflict *quickly* ("leave immediately"), *privately* ("go to this friend"), and *restoratively* ("make things right"). The *restorer* resolves conflict by approaching it with a spirit of immediacy, kindness, and grace.

Listen. Every conflict has two sides to the story, and our job is to listen to both sides to foster greater understanding. Stephen Covey said, "Seek first to understand, then to be understood."[160] Too often, we take a different approach: we *seek to make a point* so then, *they'll* understand. But that's an unwise and unfruitful strategy to build trust. Your *posture* opens the door to trust, but *listening* gives you a seat at the table of resolution.

Admit. Years ago, a conflict came to my attention between two people—I'll call them Brandy and Janet. I met with them together and quickly discovered that Brandy had done something hurtful to Janet. After a lengthy conversation, Brandy finally offered an apology: "I'm sorry if you felt that way."

Immediately I saw the problem in the apology, so I said, "Brandy, that's not really an apology." She said, "What do you mean?" I said, "You're apologizing for Janet's feelings instead of your actions." She looked perplexed, so I continued. "How Janet feels is not the problem. What you did is the problem. You need to apologize for what you did, not how Janet feels."

She got what I was saying and then offered the best apology she could muster. The meeting ended well, and both ladies hugged one another. But to my surprise, a couple of days later, Brandy called me and apologized for how she had handled the situation. She not only recognized that her response lacked humility and sincerity, but she did the most important thing you can do in any conflict: she owned it.

You can't fix what you won't own. King David said, "But I confess my sins; I am deeply sorry for what I have done" (Psalm 38:13). There's no dodging or denial in that confession, and that's the approach we must take to bring about resolution and healing. Your ability to admit and own what you've done wrong is a non-negotiable step to reestablish trust and restore the relationship.

Nurture. The old saying is true, "People don't care how much you know until they know how much you care." You can't just *say* that you care—people must *feel* that you care. This nurturing mindset places a genuine value on people. It puts the value of the relationship ahead of the need to be right.

These trust-building practices—Posture, Listen, Admit, Nurture—are the PLAN to cultivate trust so conflicts can be resolved. In addition, these practices are the PLAN to take with you into the remaining conflict-resolution strategies.

2) Choose Timing

Researcher Joseph Grenny and his colleagues at VitalSmarts discovered:

> *95 percent of a company's workforce struggles to confront their colleagues and managers about their concerns and frustrations. As a result, they engage in resource-sapping avoidance tactics, including ruminating excessively about crucial issues, complaining to others, getting angry, doing extra or unnecessary work, and avoiding the other person altogether.*

Grenny goes on to note that "employees waste an average of $1,500 and an 8-hour workday for every accountability conversation they avoid," and that eight percent of employees cost their organizations a whopping $10,000 or more because of their inability to deal with conflict.[161]

It's in your best interest—and the interest of the organization—to resolve conflict. Unfortunately, most people only address conflict in two scenarios: when it's *easy* to resolve or *too big* to ignore. When conflict resides somewhere in the middle—when it's not easy to resolve, but it hasn't turned into a full-blown crisis—we ignore the conflict or delay our response to it. But good leaders know that ignoring conflict only makes it bigger, uglier, crazier—and more expensive.

In general, the time to deal with conflict is when you can do so *quickly* and *calmly*. First, if possible, address the conflict *quickly*. The apostle Paul said, "And 'don't sin by letting anger control you.' Don't let the sun go down while you are still angry, for anger gives a foothold to the devil" (Ephesians 4:26-27). The word *foothold* means "location." Paul warns us not to let the devil use unresolved anger to acquire square footage in our soul or a guest room in our heart.

Second, deal with conflict when you can do so *calmly*. If you're raging mad, take a few minutes—or a few days—to cool down before you tackle the conflict. Proverbs 14:29 says, "Slowness to anger makes for deep understanding; a quick-tempered person stockpiles stupidity" (MSG). Here are some simple questions to ask when you're determining the right time to deal with a conflict:
- Is my current emotional state under control?
- Have I carefully considered the part I played in causing the conflict?
- Have I taken time to process how I'll address the conflict in a healthy way?
- Have I prayed through the issue at hand and for the people involved?

When you can answer "Yes" to these questions, the timing is right to address the conflict and keep it from becoming an all-out crisis.

3) Clarify Tension

You can't resolve tension unless you fully understand what's causing it. That's why I try to live by a simple rule of relationships: ask questions before jumping to conclusions. You'll never gain understanding with answers. You only gain understanding by asking questions, and then pausing to listen intently. Proverbs 18:2 provides some potent wisdom: "Fools have no interest in understanding; they only want to air their own opinions." Don't take the posture of a fool. Reserve your own opinions and take time to listen, so you can clarify the tension. Here are some helpful approaches to clarify the tension:

- "I could be wrong, but I feel like there's some underlying tension in our relationship. I wanted to take a few minutes to hear what might be bothering you."
- "I feel like I may have done something to offend you, so I wanted to see if you would help me understand what I've done and how you're feeling."
- "Recently I said something (or did something) that wasn't right. I want to own it and apologize to you for what I've done."
- "Can you help me understand what's frustrating you?"
- "Can you tell me more?"
- "What would you like to see happen in this situation?"
- "What would be a good first step from here that we could both agree on?"

Once the discussion gets going and their frustrations become clear, state back what you're hearing them say to ensure you're both on the same page. Again, your goal is to create understanding. Make observations, not accusations. "He said this" and "She said that" will only create an endless cycle of frustration and miscommunication. You may not agree with everything they say, but before you respond, ensure there's clarity about the tension.

4) Communicate Truth

Greg was a friend and a genuinely fun person. He had a big smile, a contagious laugh, and a positive attitude, and he never met a stranger. He was full of energy, incredibly social, and gifted in multiple ways. Greg only had one *big* problem: he was a habitual liar. If his lips were moving, his lies were brewing.

On one occasion, my brother Chris told me about an interaction he and another friend had with Greg. When the conversation concluded and Greg headed out the door, Chris turned to his friend and said, "Everything Greg just said was a lie."

His friend looked at him, befuddled by the comment. "Really?" he said.

"Oh, yeah, every bit of it," Chris said.

Greg was a convincing, chronic liar, and the only people who could see through his lies were those who knew him best—or those who had been burned by his conniving false promises and blatant fabrications.

We may not tell brazen lies in conflict resolution, but we can certainly dodge the truth. Why? Because we hate conflict and will look for the quickest way out from under its unnerving cloud. Unfortunately, the quickest way out is to downplay the conflict, make promises you can't keep, or exaggerate the position that will help you the most.

But there's a better path forward: pursue the truth in a trust-filled manner.

Simply put, don't talk *around* the issue; speak directly to it. This is difficult, but half-truths and outright lies will only damage trust and prolong the conflict. When you're communicating the truth, keep in mind the ABCs:

- **A**rticulate the Facts—Focus on the facts without getting sidetracked by the "-tions": assumptions, emotions, or accusations.
- **B**alance Candor and Care—Be candid about the truth while delivering it with care, dignity, and respect. As researcher Joseph Grenny observed, "The lag time for change is the same as the lag time for candor."[162] If you want things to change, it starts with the truth.

- **Cultivate Dialogue**—Communicating truth isn't a one-way speech but a two-way dialogue with the opportunity for both parties to speak and respond.

The goal of communicating truth is to bring about healing. Therefore, don't use truth as a weapon to prove a point, get your way, or crush the other person. In addition, avoid exaggerations, the blame game, and indicting words like "always" and "never."

5) Control Tone

In research conducted by The Harris Poll for Grammarly Business, four issues ranked highest in communication difficulties among knowledge workers:

- 71%—Choosing the right words to avoid offending others.
- 71%—Finding the right balance between sounding too formal and too casual.
- 63%—Spending too much time trying to convey a message in the right way.
- 56%—Feeling unsure of the correct tone for communication.[163]

While tone is specifically mentioned in the fourth-highest response, it's implied in all the responses. Not wanting to offend others, sounding too formal or casual, and conveying the message in the right way are all impacted by the tone we use.

For a powerful example of tone, look at the life of Jesus. Two remarkable attributes of Jesus are *grace* and *truth*. That perfect blend is found in the gospel of John when Jesus saved a woman from her accusers after she was caught in the act of adultery. Jesus asked the woman, "Where are your accusers? Didn't even one of them condemn you?" (John 8:10). The answer was clearly no. Then He said to her, "Neither do I. Go and sin no more" (John 8:11).

> **If your tone is one of correction, you'll put others down. But if your tone is one of connection, you'll lift others up.**

When Jesus said, "Neither do I condemn you," he extended *grace*. When He said, "Go and sin no more," He pointed her toward *truth*. Simply put, *Jesus spoke truth in the tone of grace*. We need both to resolve conflict and build thriving relationships.

Tone is established early in the conversation. If your tone is one of *correction*, you'll put others down. But if your tone is one of *connection*, you'll lift others up. Which leader do you respect the most? The one who *corrects you downward* or *coaches you upward?* The answer is obvious. The tone of connection will always outpace the tone of correction. Connection alleviates conflict while correction amplifies it.

Proverbs 15:4 shares the sound of the tone of connection: "Gentle words are a tree of life; a deceitful tongue crushes the spirit." Gentleness deflects anger and produces life. That's the connecting power of controlling your tone.

6) Collaborate Together

Just because you experience conflict with somebody doesn't mean they're your enemy. It usually means there's a misunderstanding or a misguided assumption that requires an honest conversation. If you'll have an honest conversation, collaboration toward a better and brighter future becomes possible.

Business author Alden Mills notes, "By collaborating, you are acknowledging that you need other's help, that you know they're better at something than you are, and that their ideas matter and provide value to the team."[164]

The solution to a conflict is never one-sided. It requires both parties to come together and come to an agreement. To successfully collaborate, keep three word pictures in mind:

- **The Bridge: Focus on What Unites Us**—It's easier to focus more on the conflict and less on the resolution. Rather than allowing your differences to consume you, concentrate on the bridge that unites both of you. Clearly state your common ground so that each of you recognizes your shared desire for the same outcome.
- **The Scoreboard: Make Room for Both Parties to Win**—In sports, a "shutout" happens when one team puts points on the board while the other team fails to score. That's the goal in sports, but it doesn't work in conflict resolution. Rather than focusing on a shutout, collaborate to create win-win outcomes. Work hard to ensure there's a "W" (for "Win") on both sides of the scoreboard.
- **The Footpath: Identify Your Next Steps**—Meaningful collaboration doesn't just talk about a conflict; it leads to clear and specific next steps. This happens when you ask, "Who will do what by when?" Said another way, "What will we do differently from this point forward?" A clear footpath helps you take steps toward a healthy outcome and a fruitful future.

These three word pictures—the bridge, the scoreboard, and the footpath—provide a framework for successful collaboration.

Again, this is crucial to moving forward. If you don't collaborate, you run the risk of discussing the conflict without fully resolving it.

Captain Frank Worsley navigated some of the harshest conditions on earth. His sextant, gut instincts, and careful calculations guided him through the most unforgiving seas and life-threatening situations. Similarly, the six ingredients to conflict resolution—cultivate trust, choose timing, clarify tension, communicate truth, control tone, and collaborate together—are the keys to navigating the choppy and unpredictable conflicts you'll encounter in leadership. To help you evaluate your effectiveness in resolving a recent conflict, use Leadership Tool #11: Conflict Navigator. From this tool, you'll pinpoint areas for improvement as you learn how to lead through conflict.

INSANELY PRACTICAL REFLECTION AND DISCUSSION

1. How are you challenged by the statement, "The way in which you handle conflict provides an unfiltered picture of your spiritual, emotional, and relationship maturity"?
2. How do you cultivate trust when the conflict you're experiencing has undermined trust?
3. Which of the six practices for leading through conflict is typically your biggest sticking point (cultivate trust, choose timing, clarify tension, communicate truth, control tone, or collaborate together)? What could you do to improve in this area?
4. Which tips in this chapter would help you successfully resolve a conflict you're facing right now?

LEADERSHIP TOOL #11
Conflict Navigator

Use the chart below to describe a conflict you've recently encountered. Then, use the Green/Yellow/Red rating system to evaluate how successfully you implemented the six practices to resolve the conflict. At the bottom of the chart, write down your top two lessons to improve future conflict resolution.

Write a brief description below of a conflict you've recently encountered.			
Use the Green/Yellow/Red rating system below to evaluate how effectively you used the six practices to resolve the conflict you described above.			
CONFLICT RESOLUTION PRACTICE	RESOLUTION RATING		
	Green	Yellow	Red
PRACTICE #1: CULTIVATE TRUST			
My posture in the conflict was that of a restorer.			
I listened to understand during the conflict.			
I admitted what I did wrong.			
I nurtured my value for the relationship over being right.			
PRACTICE #2: CHOOSE TIMING			
My emotional state was under control before we talked.			
I was ready to own my part in causing the conflict.			
I prepared in advance to address the conflict in a good way.			
I first prayed about the conflict and for the people involved.			

PRACTICE #3: CLARIFY TENSION			
I carefully considered how I'd start the conversation.			
I listened carefully without getting defensive.			
I sought to understand and avoided making accusations.			
I successfully clarified the real issue at hand.			
PRACTICE #4: COMMUNICATE TRUTH			
I articulated the facts I needed to communicate.			
I practiced the appropriate balance of candor with care.			
I cultivated dialogue instead of one-way communication.			
PRACTICE #5: CONTROL TONE			
I spoke in a healthy and grace-filled tone the entire time.			
I spoke in a connecting tone rather than a correcting tone.			
I was coaching upward rather than correcting downward.			
PRACTICE #6: COLLABORATE TOGETHER			
I acknowledged what united us.			
I actively sought a win-win resolution.			
I ended by identifying our next steps to move forward.			
LESSONS TO IMPROVE HOW I LEAD THROUGH CONFLICT			

Download the Conflict Navigator at insanelypracticalleadership.com.

CHAPTER 12

HOW TO COACH OTHERS

"A 'coach' remains something, or someone, who carries a valued person from where they are to where they want to be."
—Kevin Hall

"Stephen, we're a great family, but we suck organizationally."

Those are the words Jason shared with me in our first coaching conversation as he described the church he planted several years earlier. He was grateful for their burgeoning growth, and he loved his team and their unwavering commitment to the church's mission, but Jason's comment made his pain point abundantly clear.

Jason is a great communicator, and he's never short on vision and ideas. On top of that, the church has a solid Sunday morning experience, along with a great group of devoted volunteers. But Jason's frustration with his lack of organizational acumen was reaching a tipping point.

I continued asking questions to ensure I understood the depths of his struggle and how I could help. "Our team is great," he said, "and we love each other, but I haven't done a good job developing leaders." Jason even cited examples of good leaders who had come and gone, underutilized for their God-given leadership capacity.

As the conversation evolved, Jason began to describe the challenges of working with a mix of paid and volunteer staff. "How do I get them to own their responsibilities independent of me?" he asked. "What changes do I need to make in our staffing structure as we grow?" Then, he asked about staff meetings, the content of those meetings, and how to maximize their effectiveness. He peppered me with questions, and I returned the favor by asking even more questions. The more we talked, the clearer the picture became.

I love coaching leaders like Jason. He's hungry to grow, and he's willing to try anything to elevate his effectiveness. He doesn't make excuses or cast blame, and he musters the courage to make tough decisions. When you have the desire to learn *and* the will to change, the sky is the limit.

In the remainder of that single coaching conversation, a plan emerged to create clear role descriptions, develop quarterly goals with each team member, establish systems of accountability, and restructure existing meetings to better serve his staff. It was a breakthrough moment for Jason, and it helped him gain the insight he needed to get from where he was to where he wanted to be. Most importantly, he implemented the entire plan, and it has transformed how his team functions.

FROM HERE TO THERE

In his book, *Aspire*, Kevin Hall provides some insightful backstory on the origin of the word *coach*. A village named "Kocs" in old Hungary produced horse-drawn vehicles used to comfortably transport royalty between Budapest and Vienna. These carriages became known as "coaches," borrowing their name from the township where they were designed. Their comfortable design made travel across the bumpy roads in fifteenth-century Europe more bearable.

Over time, the term "coach" was applied to other modes of transportation, such as the stagecoach, railway coach, and motorcoach. Kevin Hall observed this:

> *However far-reaching and prevalent the word has become since the first coach rolled out of production in Kocs, the meaning has not changed. A "coach" remains something, or someone, who carries a valued person from where they are to where they want to be.*[165]

Simply put, coaches help you get from *here* to *there*.

> **Coaching isn't just something you need; it's also something you should do.**

Coaches are a staple in the arena of sports. Golfers and tennis players have coaches because they want to get better and maximize their talent, and professional teams have *multiple* coaches, each focused on a unique aspect of the game, as well as the skills necessary to win. But coaching isn't just for sports. To go from "here to there," leaders need coaches too.

Citing Gallup's research of more than twenty-seven million employees worldwide, Brandon Busteed makes a candid analysis to becoming successful in leadership: "The single most important thing you can do to help ensure your future success is to find a great manager or a great adviser and mentor."[166] Coaches take a serious interest in your growth and use their skills to draw God-given potential out of you.

However, coaching isn't just something you *need*; it's also something you should *do*. Coaching is a leadership skill. It's an indispensable tool in your leadership toolbox, and if you hone this skill with precision, you'll catalyze your ability to help others grow.

What does a leadership coach do? Coaching expert Keith Webb observes:

Coaching involves listening to others, asking questions to deepen thinking, allowing others to find their own solutions, and doing it all in a way that makes people feel empowered and responsible enough to take action.[167]

That's a great summary of a coach's skills and objectives as they guide people toward optimal outcomes. You can do the same.

HOW TO COACH OTHERS

Coaching is an entire industry, and I would encourage you to take advantage of the wealth of training and resources available to become a proficient coach. In addition, I want to provide an insanely practical framework to help you develop your coaching skills. I call it AIM.

Good leadership coaches take **AIM** at the potential in people. Simply put, they coach leaders toward **A**ssessment, **I**nsight, and **M**ovement. Each key forms a practical roadmap to guide effective coaching conversations and catalyze personal and professional growth.

ASSESSMENT

Coaching begins with *Assessment*. You can't help someone remove barriers, increase their leadership capacity, or grow their organizational effectiveness unless you first assess where they are and what they need. That's what I did with Jason. I asked questions to assess his biggest challenges and understand his specific context. Without assessment, you won't connect with the person you're coaching, and you'll risk prescribing solutions to problems that don't exist. There are two ways to provide assessment.

Ask Questions. A coaching session usually begins with some welcoming comments and casual conversation. A simple question like, "How's it going?" and "What's new since we last talked?" is a great way to start. This helps you connect with the individual and discover what's happening in their life. If it's a new team member, learn a bit of their story before you dive into their needs as a leader. Your goal is to build rapport and express a genuine interest in them.

Once you connect, shift the conversation by saying, "What do you hope to gain from our time together?" or "What areas of your leadership would you like to discuss today?" or "What would you like to focus on this afternoon?" You want to identify their goal for the coaching conversation. Sometimes, this takes several follow-up questions, especially if they're struggling to articulate a specific need. Be patient and keep exploring. Whatever you do, resist the urge to dole out ideas and solutions. As you'll see, many of the answers to their problems will actually come from them (not you).

Administer Assessments. A second way to provide assessment is to administer assessment tools. For example, if the person you're coaching wants to leverage their strengths for greater organizational impact, administer a tool like *CliftonStrengths*.[168] If they want to improve their leadership skills, administer the Leadership Practices Inventory.[169] Good assessment tools provide greater context, as well as a baseline for the coaching conversation.

The two goals of assessment are *connection* and *clarity*. You want to *connect* with the individual and gain *clarity* about their needs, struggles, and goals. As you use questions to build connection and increase clarity, you'll be equipped to move to the second key.

INSIGHT

Insight is where a team member discovers perspective, wisdom, and ideas to take measurable steps forward in their leadership journey. The majority of your conversation will happen here, and it's where the person you're coaching will discover answers to their biggest challenges. As a coach, you can facilitate this discovery process with two strategies.

Pull Out. The first strategy is to *pull* the insight out of the person you're coaching by asking good questions. For example, if a team member shares a specific struggle with you, then ask, "How have you dealt with this struggle in the past?" or "What options do you have to move forward?" If they're trying to get clear about a vision for the future, say, "What have you been dreaming about lately?" or "What do you think is possible in the next twelve months?" or "What would add the greatest value to your department right now?" If they're frustrated with a coworker, ask, "How is this frustration impacting you and your work?" and "Can you boil this frustration down to one or two sentences?" Then you might ask, "Have you talked to them about it?" or "What have you found to be the best way to approach them?"

> **Good coaches add insight without becoming the only source of insight.**

As they answer your questions, dig deeper. You might say, "Tell me more," "Unpack that for me," "Help me understand," or "What are the pros and cons of this solution?" Every question puts you one step closer to pulling the solution out of the person you're coaching. Why is this important? Because if *they* come up with the solution, they're much more likely to *own it*.

Pour In. The second strategy to surface key insights is to *pour* into the person you're coaching. In these moments, you'll temporarily remove your coaching hat and put on a mentoring hat. Coaches *pull out*, but mentors *pour in*. Then, share a thought, an insight, an idea, or a perspective that could help them get unstuck and move forward. You're simply offering a different perspective to help them experience an aha moment.

Author and coaching expert Terry Walling refers to this method as "Breakthru Coaching." During a Breakthru Coaching Event, I heard Terry say:

> *Breakthrough results from the timely combination of coaching and mentoring. . . . The coach's role is to facilitate discovery in the leader's life. At strategic moments in the conversation, coaches need to dispense key leadership development insights to help facilitate the breakthrough that a leader is seeking.*

I used this strategy with Jason. I shared some helpful tools with him and guided him through their application in his context.

After you *pour in*, put your coaching hat back on and begin to *pull out*. After all, if you do all a team member's thinking for them, you'll make them dependent on you. Good coaches add insight without becoming the *only* source of insight.

A mixture of *pulling out* and *pouring in* will help the people you're coaching discover the insights and experience the breakthroughs they need to improve and advance. That brings us to the final coaching key.

MOVEMENT

Your goal isn't just to help the person you're coaching come up with great ideas or fresh insights. You also want them to chart a pathway to progress and take their first steps. Movement requires two keys.

Identify Action Steps. The first key is to help the person you're coaching turn their insights into specific action steps. Without action, they'll never apply what they're learning. To create this movement, ask, "What do you think is the first step you should take between now and the next time we meet?" Or say, "You've offered some great insights in our time together. What action step do you want to tackle first?"

The key is to ensure the action step is achievable before your next meeting. If the step is too big, their lack of progress will frustrate them. Help them break their goal into clear, measurable, bite-sized steps that can be reached in a reasonable amount of time.

Give Permission and Encouragement. A common roadblock people experience in the coaching process is a lack of confidence. That's when good coaches give them permission to act. To be clear, they don't technically need your permission to move forward. However, when they're struggling with self-doubt, uncertainty, or imposter syndrome, a permission-giving statement can make all the difference. For example, you'll bolster their confidence when you say, "You've got this inside of you. You can do this. I believe in you." When they know you believe in them, it helps them believe in themselves.

Another key to Movement is to speak words of encouragement to the person you're coaching as they implement action steps. Deliberately affirm their efforts, celebrate their progress, and encourage them to keep going. Mother Teresa once said, "Kind words can be short and easy to speak, but their echoes are endless."[170] Your words of encouragement are the endless echoes that keep people moving after they leave the coaching session.

Movement helps the people you coach not only identify a path forward but stick with their solution. It puts wind in their sails as they act on their insights.

MAXIMIZING YOUR COACHING SKILLS

Coaching is a skill, but you can apply this skill in multiple contexts. You can use it during one-on-one meetings with your staff. You can leverage it in meetings with volunteers, interns, and friends. You don't have to engage in a formal coaching relationship to use the skill of coaching. Everybody has goals, roadblocks, and setbacks. As you cultivate the skill of coaching, you'll be able to employ it as needed to help others move forward.

These three keys—Assessment, Insight, and Movement—will help you take AIM at the potential in others. As you coach them, you'll draw potential out of them and pour confidence into them. You'll help them close the gap between who they are and who they can become. Leadership Tool #12: AIM Coaching Guide provides helpful questions to facilitate coaching conversations. Put it to work and watch the people around you grow to their full potential.

INSANELY PRACTICAL REFLECTION AND DISCUSSION

1. How have you personally benefited from coaching? In what way would coaching help you become a better leader right now?
2. How does it feel to think of yourself as a coach?
3. How does the AIM Coaching Model help you think about coaching? What is most helpful about the model?
4. Who is someone you could begin coaching right now? What questions would be helpful to ask in your coaching conversations?

LEADERSHIP TOOL #12
AIM Coaching Guide

Use the AIM Coaching Guide to help you take AIM at the potential in others and coach them toward their goals and objectives. These sample questions will help you put the AIM Coaching Model to work.

AIM COACHING GUIDE
Below are sample questions you can ask in a coaching conversation. These questions use the AIM Coaching Model to help you guide an individual toward Assessment, Insight, and Movement. With this model, a coach can take AIM at an individual's potential by helping them clarify their goals, come up with practical solutions, and move forward to achieve their objectives.
ASSESSMENT QUESTIONS
1. How's it going?
2. How have things been since our last meeting?
3. What progress have you made on your last assignment?
4. What would you like to talk about today?
5. What do you hope to gain from our time together today?
INSIGHT QUESTIONS
6. How have you dealt with this struggle in the past?
7. What do you think is the root cause of this problem?
8. What surprised you most about this challenge?
9. What worked and didn't work in your previous response to this challenge?
10. What would be the best outcome in this situation?
11. How could you achieve that outcome?
12. Can you unpack that for me a bit more?
13. What options do you have to move forward?
14. What's another option to reach this goal?
15. How would you advise someone with this same challenge?
16. What would make the biggest difference right now?
17. Who could help you reach this goal?

18.	What might be the long-term benefits or consequences of these options?
19.	How might that affect those closest to you?
20.	What's holding you back?
MOVEMENT QUESTIONS	
21.	How can you turn these insights into an action step?
22.	What would be a good first step to move forward?
23.	When will you talk to your team about this?
24.	What part of this strategy would you like to accomplish before our next meeting?
25.	What was your biggest takeaway from our time together today?

Download the AIM Coaching Guide at
insanelypracticalleadership.com.

ENDNOTES

1 Randall J. Beck and Jim Harter, "Why Great Managers Are So Rare," *Gallup*, 21 July 2023, https://www.gallup.com/workplace/231593/why-great-managers-rare.aspx.
2 "State of the American Manager Report," *Gallup*, 21 Oct. 2015, https://www.gallup.com/services/182216/state-american-manager-report.aspx.
3 John Maxwell, *Developing the Leader Within You* (Nashville: Thomas Nelson, 1993), IX.
4 Stephen Blandino, *GO! Starting a Personal Growth Revolution* (Scotts Valley: CreateSpace, 2012).
5 Ken Blanchard and Mark Miller, *Great Leaders Grow: Becoming a Leader for Life* (San Francisco: Berrett-Koehler Publishers, 2012), 94.
6 Michael Hyatt, *Your Best Year Ever: A Five-Step Plan for Achieving Your Most Important Goals* (Grand Rapids: Baker Books, 2018), 32.
7 Samuel R. Chand, *Leadership Pain: The Classroom for Growth* (Nashville: Thomas Nelson, 2015), 15.
8 Erwin Raphael McManus, *Mind Shift: It Doesn't Take a Genius to Think Like One* (New York: Convergent Books, 2023), 62.
9 John Maxwell, *Developing the Leader Within You* (Nashville: Thomas Nelson, 2005).
10 John Maxwell, *The 21 Irrefutable Laws of Leadership: Follow Them and People Will Follow You* (Nashville: HarperCollins, 2007).
11 Blandino, *Go!*
12 Jim Collins, quoted by John Maxwell, *Leadershift: 11 Essential Changes Every Leader Must Embrace* (New York: HarperCollins Leadership, 2019), 75.
13 "What Happened in 1984," *On This Day*, https://www.onthisday.com/date/1984.
14 Greg McKeown, "How to Simplify Your Life in 5 Minutes a Day," *Greg McKeown Blog*, 16 Oct. 2024, http://gregmckeown.com/blog/simplify-life-5-minutes-day/#sthash.0mNBFQyI.dpuf.
15 Mother Teresa interview with Dan Rather, as quoted in Ron Mehl, *What God Whispers in the Night* (Sisters: Multnomah, 2000), 97.

16 Richard Foster, *Celebration of Discipline, Special Anniversary Edition: The Path to Spiritual Growth* (New York: HarperCollins, 2018), xv.

17 Ryan Skoog, Peter Greer, and Cameron Doolittle, *Lead With Prayer* (New York: Faith Words, 2024), 132.

18 Bobby Clinton and Richard Clinton, *Leaders on Leadership: Wisdom, Advice and Encouragement on the Art of Leading God's People,* ed. George Barna (Grand Rapids: Baker Books, 1998), 149-182.

19 Steve Moore, *The Top 10 Leadership Conversations in the Bible* (Atlanta: nexleader, 2017), 33.

20 Red Huber, "Looking back at Winter Park's famous sinkhole," *Orlando Sentinel*, 21 Dec. 2018, https://www.orlandosentinel.com/os-fla360-looking-back-at-winter-parks-famous-sinkhole-20121113-story.html.

21 Richard Luscombe, "Florida's most famous sinkhole, *The Guardian*, 14 Aug 2013, https://www.theguardian.com/world/2013/aug/14/florida-most-famous-sinkhole.

22 Luscombe.

23 "Sinkhole creates new Florida lake: History of Lake Rose in Winter Park," *Fox 35 Orlando*, 18 Aug 2022, https://www.fox35orlando.com/news/sinkhole-creates-new-florida-history-of-lake-rose-in-winter-park.

24 Water Science School, "Sinkholes," *USGS,* 9 Jun 2018, https://www.usgs.gov/special-topics/water-science-school/science/sinkholes.

25 Lance Witt, *Replenish: Leading from a Healthy Soul* (Grand Rapids: Baker Books, 2011), 19.

26 Bob Goff, quoted by Brad Lomenick, *The Catalyst Leader: 8 Essentials for Becoming a Change Maker* (Nashville: Thomas Nelson, 2013), 147.

27 Richard Foster, *Celebration of Discipline: The Path to Spiritual Growth* (San Francisco: HarperCollins, 1998), 7.

28 Steve Moore, *The Dream Cycle: Leveraging the Power of Personal Growth* (Fishers: Wesleyan Publishing House, 2004), 137.

29 John Ronald Reuel Tolkien, *The Hobbit* (Boston: Houghton Mifflin Harcourt, 2012).

30 J. R. R. Tolkien, *The Letters of J.R.R. Tolkien*, ed. Humphrey Carpenter (Boston: Houghton Mifflin, 1981), 362.

31 J. R. R. Tolkien, *Lord of the Rings* (United Kingdom: Allen & Unwin, 1954-1955).

32 Wayne Cordeiro, *Leading on Empty* (Bloomington: Bethany House Publishers, 2009), Chapter 9.

33 Andrew Carnegie, quoted by Maxwell Leadership, Twitter post, March 7, 2018, 11:06 am, https://x.com/Maxwell_Leaders/status/971416835341082625.

34 There, we see nineteen kings in Israel's history from Jeroboam to Hoshea. Of these kings, we find a variation of this description linking them to the sins of Jeroboam: King Nadab (1 Kings 15:26); King Baasha (1 Kings 16:2); King Zimri (1 Kings 16:19); King Omri (1 Kings 16:26); King Ahab (1 Kings 16:31); King Ahab (2 Kings 3:3); King Jehu (2 Kings 10:31); King Jehoahaz (2 Kings 13:1-2); King Jehoash (2 Kings 13:10-11); King Jeroboam II (2 Kings 14:23-24); King Zechariah (2 Kings 15:8-9); King Menahem (2 Kings 15:17-18); King Pekahiah (2 Kings 15:23-24); King Pekah (2 Kings 15:27-28). Three other kings are not specifically linked to King Jeroboam, but Scripture describes them as kings who led Israel to sin (which was part of the description given to King Jeroboam) or kings who followed the example of previous kings which are linked to Jeroboam's sin: King Elah (1 Kings 16:13); King Ahaziah (1 Kings 22:51-53, 2 Kings 8:27); King Hoshea (2 Kings 17:1-2). One king—King Shallum—only reigned one month because he was assassinated. There is not enough information to describe him as any different than the previous kings (2 Kings 15:13-15).

35 Sandra Sadek, "Bars have boomed in Fort Worth's West 7th neighborhood. So has the crime rate," *Fort Worth Report,* 28 Aug 2022, https://fortworthreport.org/2022/08/28/bars-have-boomed-in-fort-worths-west-7th-neighborhood-so-has-the-crime-rate/.

36 Jessica Priest, "Mayor explains increased police presence in West 7th district on weekends," *Fort Worth Report,* 11 Oct 2021, https://fortworthreport.org/2021/10/11/mayor-explains-increased-police-presence-in-west-7th-district-on-weekends/.

37 Mark Batterson, Richard Foth, and Susanna Foth Aughtmon, *A Trip Around the Sun: Turning Your Everyday Life into the Adventure of a Lifetime* (Grand Rapids: Baker Books, 2015), 124.

38 Dan Reiland, *Confident Leader! Become One, Stay One* (Nashville: Thomas Nelson, 2020), 15.

39 "Is there a reason you're late, or is it just an excuse?" *CareerBuilder,* https://www.careerbuilder.com/advice/blog/is-there-a-reason-youre-late-or-is-it-just-an-excuse.

40 R. T. Kendall, as quoted by Mark Batterson, *If: Trading Your If Only Regrets for God's What If Possibilities* (Grand Rapids, MI: Baker Books, 2015), 164.

41 Matthew S. Olson, Derek van Bever, and Seth Verry, "When Growth Stalls," *Harvard Business Review,* 21 Dec. 2023, https://hbr.org/2008/03/when-growth-stalls#:~:text=Eventually%20they%20harden%20into%20orthodoxy,longer%20politic%20to%20debate%20them.

42 Brad Lomenick, *H3: Be Humble. Stay Hungry. Always Hustle* (Nashville: Nelson Books, 2015), 94.

43 Olson, Bever, and Verry, "When Growth Stalls."

44 Andrew Carnegie, quoted by Hans Finzel, *The Top Ten Mistakes Leaders Make* (Colorado Springs: David C. Cook, 2007), 83.

45 "Craig Groeschel Leadership Podcast," *Open Network,* https://open.life.church/training/216-craig-groeschel-leadership-podcast-creating-an-empowering-culture-part-2.

46 Captain D. Michael Abrashoff, *It's Your Ship: Management Techniques from the Best Damn Ship in the Navy* (New York: Warner Books, 2002), 33.

47 Abrashoff, 107.

48 Brian Tracy, "The Value of Long-term Perspective," *American Management Association,* 24 Mar. 2020, https://www.amanet.org/articles/the-value-of-a-long-term-perspective/.

49 Daniel S. Harkavy, *Becoming a Coaching Leader: The Proven Strategy for Building Your Own Team of Champions* (Nashville: Thomas Nelson, 2007).

50 Stephen Blandino, *Do Good Works: Am I Doing What I Was Made to Do?* (Scotts Valley: CreateSpace, 2017).

51 John Maxwell, *Don't Manage Your Time—Manage Your Life* (New York: HarperCollins, 2012).

52 Stephen R. Covey, quoted by Chris McChesney, Sean Covey, and Jim Huling, *The 4 Disciplines of Execution* (New York: Simon & Schuster, 2012), 30.

53 Michael Hyatt, *Free to Focus: A Total Productivity System to Achieve More by Doing Less* (Grand Rapids: Baker Books, 2019), 191-202.

54 Stacy Jo Dixon, "Daily time spent on social networking by internet users worldwide from 2012 to 2024," *Statista,* 10 Apr 2024, https://www.statista.com/statistics/433871/daily-social-media-usage-worldwide/.

55 FWTX staff, "We're No. 12! Fort Worth Population Continues To Go Boom," *Fortworth,* 16 May 2024, https://fwtx.com/news/we-re-no-12-fort-worth-population-continues-to-go-boom/#:~:text=Fort%20Worth%2C%20with%20a%20population,No.%2010%20Jacksonville%2C%20Florida.

56 Stephen Blandino, "Eight Keys to Effective Decision Making," *Influence Magazine,* May/June 2019, MIC_Decision_Making_Discussion_Guide2_May-June_2018.pdf.

57 John Maxwell, *The 21 Irrefutable Laws of Leadership* (New York: HarperCollins Leadership, 2022), 98-99.

58 Bryan Stevenson, "Catherine Coleman Flowers," *TIME,* 13 Apr 2023, https://time.com/collection/100-most-influential-people-2023/6269958/catherine-coleman-flowers/.

59 Robert E. Picirilli, *Paul the Apostle: Missionary, Martyr, Theologian* (Chicago: Moody Publishers, 2017), 31-32.

60 John Pollock, *The Apostle: A Life of Paul* (Colorado Springs: David C. Cook, 2012), 17-18.

61 "Do Paul's Missions Leave Us With a Geographic Pattern to Follow–Ask Pastor John Podcast," *Desiring God,* 25 Apr. 2018, https://www.desiringgod.org/interviews/do-pauls-missions-leave-us-with-a-geographic-pattern-to-follow.

62 Neil Cole, "How Many Churches Did The Apostle Paul Start?" *ChurchPlanting.com,* 24 Feb 2020, https://churchplanting.com/how-many-churches-did-the-apostle-paul-start/.

63 N. T. Wright, *Paul: A Biography* (New York: Harper One, 2020), 69.
64 Neil Cole, *Journeys to Significance: Charting a Leadership Course from the Life of Paul* (San Francisco: Jossey-Bass, 2011), 30.
65 Kevin Myers and John C. Maxwell, *Homerun: Learn God's Game Plan for Life and Leadership* (New York: FaithWords, 2014), 113.
66 Mark Batterson, *Double Blessing: How to Get It. How to Give It* (Colorado Springs: Multnomah, 2019), 22.
67 David B. Capes, "Paul's Co-Workers," *A Word In Edgewise*, 24 Jan. 2013, https://davidbcapes.com/articles/brief-articles/pauls-co-workers/#:~:text=Depending%20upon%20how%20broadly%20the,Timothy%2C%20Titus%2C%20Tychichus).
68 Maxwell, *The 21 Irrefutable Laws*, 181.
69 James Kouzes and Barry Posner, *The Leadership Challenge: How to Make Extraordinary Things Happen in Organizations* (Hoboken: John Wiley & Sons, 2023), 7.
70 Mel Gibson, *Braveheart* (May 19, 1995; Hollywood: Paramount Pictures).
71 Billy Graham, quoted by Richard Stearns, *Lead Like It Matters to God: Values-Driven Leadership in a Success-Driven World* (Downers Grove: InterVarsity Press, 2021), 120.
72 Picirilli, 14-15.
73 Pollock, *The Apostle: A Life of Paul*, 20.
74 Ken Blanchard and Mark Miller, *Great Leaders Grow: Becoming a Leader for Life* (San Francisco: Berrett-Koehler Publishers, Inc., 2012), 11.
75 Sarah Roller, "Who Were The Crew of Shackleton's Endurance Expedition?" *History Hit*, 9 Mar 2022, https://www.historyhit.com/the-crew-of-shackletons-endurance-expedition/.
76 Alfred Lansing, *Endurance: Shackleton's Incredible Voyage* (New York: Basic Books, 2014), 17.
77 Leanne Pooley, *Shackleton's Captain* (2012; Mainz: ZDF Studios).
78 Lansing, *Endurance*, 35.
79 Lansing, 53.
80 Pooley, *Shackleton's Captain*.
81 Lansing, *Endurance*, 140.
82 Morrell and Capparell, 72.
83 Lansing, *Endurance*, 262.
84 Lansing, 268.
85 Julia Buckley, "'Like going to the moon': The world's most terrifying ocean crossing," *CNN travel*, 5 Feb. 2024, https://www.cnn.com/travel/article/drake-passage-rough-sea-scn/index.html.
86 Lansing, *Endurance*, 299.
87 Lansing, 293.
88 Lansing, 302.
89 Lansing, 304.

90 Lansing, 321.

91 Pooley, *Shackleton's Captain*.

92 Lansing, *Endurance*, 350.

93 Martha Lagace, "Ernest Shackleton: The Entrepreneur of Survival," *Harvard Business School*, 5 Dec 2014, https://www.hbs.edu/news/articles/Pages/shackleton-anniversary.aspx.

94 James Hunter, *The Servant: A Simple Story About the True Essence of Leadership* (New York: Crown Publishing Group, 1998), 28.

95 Nancy Koehn, "Why Ernest Shackleton Is Still Relevant Today," *Shackleton*, 10 Aug 2021, https://shackleton.com/en-us/blogs/articles/why-ernest-shackleton-is-still-relevant-today.

96 "Map," *National Library of Scotland*, https://www.nls.uk/learning-zone/geography-and-exploration/shackleton-and-wordie/map/#:~:text=This%20map%20shows%20the%20proposed,coast%20of%20the%20Ross%20Sea.

97 Morrell and Capparell, *Shackleton's Way*, 56.

98 Morrell and Capparell, 69.

99 Morrell and Capparell, 84.

100 Morrell and Capparell, 89.

101 Morrell and Capparell, 91.

102 Michael Smith, "What Made Shackleton A Great Leader?" *Shackleton*, 5 Feb 2020, https://shackleton.com/en-us/blogs/articles/shackleton-great-leader.

103 Koehn, "Why Ernest Shackleton Is Still Relevant Today."

104 Tom King, "How a 5-String Banjo Saved the Shackleton Expedition," *Banjo Hangout*, 8 Oct 2013, https://www.banjohangout.org/blog/30818.

105 Morrell and Capparell, *Shackleton's Way*, 143-144.

106 Morrell and Capparell, 133.

107 "Booker T. Washington," *Bible.org*, 2 Feb. 2009, https://bible.org/node/10525.

108 Stephen Blandino, "The Two Sides of Servant Leadership: Finding a Healthy and Biblical Balance," *Influence Magazine*, 14 Feb 2020, https://influencemagazine.com/en/Practice/The-Two-Sides-of-Servant-Leadership.

109 "Pharisees, Sadducees & Essenes," *Ancient Jewish History*, www.jewishvirtuallibrary.org/pharisees-sadducees-and-essenes#:~:text=The%20Pharisees%20believed%20that%20God,prayer%20and%20assembly%20in%20synagogues.

110 John MacArthur, *Matthew 8-15, The MacArthur New Testament Commentary* (Chicago: Moody Press, 1985), 430-431.

111 Mara L. Pratt, "An Anecdote of Washington," *Heritage History*, https://www.heritage-history.com/index.php?c=read&author=pratt&book=ahs2&story=washington.

112 Ramecesse Rhau, "Change," *Medium*, 1 Sept. 2019, https://medium.com/@rrhau/we-cannot-become-what-we-want-by-remaining-what-we-are-max-depree-d776685d6e61.

113 William E. Wallace, ed., *Life and Early Works (Michelangelo: Selected Scholarship in English)* (New York: Garland Publishing, 1995), 233.

114 Moore, *The Top 10 Leadership Conversations in the Bible*, 140.

115 Warren Wiersbe, *Be Loyal: Following the King of Kings, NT Commentary, Matthew* (Colorado Springs: David C. Cook, 1980), 209.

116 John Dickson, *Humilitas: A Lost Key to Life, Love, and Leadership* (Grand Rapids: Zondervan, 2011), 24.

117 John Stott, quoted by Samuel R. Chand, *Leadership Pain*, 176.

118 Adoniram Judson, quoted by John Maxwell in *Leadership*, 64.

119 Michele Morin, "What Does It Look like to Serve Others as Jesus Served?" *Living Our Days*, 31 July 2023, michelemorin.net/2023/08/02/what-does-it-look-like-to-serve-others-as-jesus-served/#:~:text=When%20writer%20Elisabeth%20Elliot%20sensed,somebody%20treats%20you%20like%20one.".

120 John Uri, "35 Years Ago: Remembering Challenger and Her Crew," *Explore*, 28 Jan 2021, https://www.nasa.gov/history/35-years-ago-remembering-challenger-and-her-crew/.

121 Uri, "35 Years Ago."

122 Vanessa Dean Arnold and John C. Malley, "Communication: The Missing Link in the Challenger Disaster," *ABC* 51, no. 4 (December 1988): 12, https://doi.org/10.1177/108056998805100404?journalCode=bcqc.

123 Howard Berkes, "30 Years After Explosion, Challenger Engineer Still Blames Himself," *NPR*, 28 Jan 2016, https://www.npr.org/sections/thetwo-way/2016/01/28/464744781/30-years-after-disaster-challenger-engineer-still-blames-himself.

124 "Chapter V: The Contributing Cause of the The Accident," *Report of the Presidential Commission on the Space Shuttle Challenger Accident*, https://history.nasa.gov/rogersrep/v1ch5.htm.

125 Michael Hyatt, *No-Fail Communication: 13 Workplace Communication Problems and How to Fix Them* (Nashville: Michael Hyatt & Company, 2020), 17.

126 Hyatt, *No-Fail Communication*, 26.

127 "State of Business Communication in 2023: Poor Workplace Communication Sinking Productivity and Performance," *Agility PR Solutions*, 27 Feb. 2023, www.agilitypr.com/pr-news/public-relations/state-of-business-comms-in-2023-poor-workplace-communication-sinking-productivity-and-performance/.

128 Jon Favreau, *Elf* (Nov. 7, 2003; Burbank, CA: Warner Brothers).

129 Mark Twain, as quoted in Denis Ledoux, "Are You Using Lightning Bug Words?" *The Memoir Network*, 23 Aug. 2021, https://thememoirnetwork.com/lightning-bug-words/.

130 Arnold and Malley, "Communication," 12.

131 Dom Barnard, "Average Speaking Rate and Words per Minute," *VirtualSpeech*, 8 Nov 2022, https://virtualspeech.com/blog/average-speaking-rate-words-per-minute.

132 *The New Adventures of Winnie the Pooh,* Stephen Anderson and Don Hall (January 17, 1988; Burbank, CA: Walt Disney Animation Studios), Television.
133 The State of Business Communication 2023 Report, 27.
134 Mark Miller, *Smart Leadership: Four Simple Choices to Scale Your Impact* (Dallas: Matt Holt Books, 2022), 159.
135 Albert Einstein, as quoted by Mark Miller, 137.
136 Robert K. Greenleaf, *Servant Leadership: A Journey Into the Nature of Legitimate Power and Greatness* (Mahwah: Paulist Press, 1977), 314.
137 Adam Hayes, "The Human Attention Span," *wyzowl,* 29 May 2024, https://www.wyzowl.com/human-attention-span/.
138 Emily Dreibelbis, "Americans Check Their Phones an Alarming Number of Times Per Day," *PCMag,* 19 May 2023, https://www.pcmag.com/news/americans-check-their-phones-an-alarming-number-of-times-per-day.
139 Allan and Barbara Pease, "The Definitive Book of Body Language," *The New York Times,* 24 Sept. 2006, https://www.nytimes.com/2006/09/24/books/chapters/0924-1st-peas.html.
140 Peter Drucker, as quoted by John Maxwell, *25 Ways to Win with People* (New York: HarperCollins Leadership, 2005), 99.
141 Discover our Shared Heritage Travel Itinerary Series, "Nevada and Arizona: Hoover Dam," *National Park Service,* https://www.nps.gov/articles/nevada-and-arizona-hoover-dam.htm.
142 Anna Skinner, "Hoover Dam Brings Electricity to 1.3 Million—It's At Risk of Shutting Down," *Newsweek,* 21 Nov 2022, https://www.newsweek.com/hoover-dam-brings-electricity-1-million-risk-shutting-down-1760762.
143 Patty Rasmussen, "Fallout: What Would Happen if the Hoover Dam Broke?" *howstuffworks,* 14 Aug 2023, https://science.howstuffworks.com/engineering/structural/hoover-dam-broke.htm#pt1.
144 Viktor Frankl, as quoted by Mark Miller, *Smart Leadership,* 21.
145 Cheryl Bachelder, *Dare to Serve: How to Drive Superior Results by Serving Others* (Oakland: Berrett-Koehler Publishers, 2015), 87.
146 Miller, *Smart Leadership,* 124.
147 William H. Whyte, quoted by quoteresearch, "The Biggest Problem in Communication Is the Illusion That It Has Taken Place," *Quote Investigator,* 31 Aug 2014, https://quoteinvestigator.com/2014/08/31/illusion/.
148 "Who was Frank Worsley?" *Antarctic Heritage Trust,* 10 Feb. 2022, https://nzaht.org/who-was-frank-worsley/.
149 "Who was Frank Worsley?" *Antarctic Heritage Trust,* https://nzaht.org/who-was-frank-worsley/.
150 Morrell and Capparell, *Shackleton's Way,* 60.

151 Kieran Mulvaney, "The Stunning Survival Story of Ernest Shackleton and His Endurance Crew," *History*, 2 May 2024, https://www.history.com/news/shackleton-endurance-survival.
152 Lansing, *Endurance*, 235-236.
153 Lansing, 244.
154 Lansing, 282-285.
155 Lansing, 288.
156 Pooley, *Shackleton's Captain*.
157 Daniella McCahey, "Endurance Captain Frank Worsley, Shackleton's Gifted Navigator, Knew How to Stay the Course," *The Conversation*, 18 Jan. 2024, https://theconversation.com/endurance-captain-frank-worsley-shackletons-gifted-navigator-knew-how-to-stay-the-course-179045.
158 Pooley, *Shackleton's Captain*.
159 "Who was Frank Worsley?"
160 Stephen R. Covey, *The 7 Habits of Highly Effective People: Powerful Lessons in Persona Change* (New York: Free Press, 2004).
161 Joseph Grenny, "Eliminating the Costs of Conflict Avoidance," *ATD Home*, 22 Jul 2013, https://www.td.org/content/atd-blog/eliminating-the-costs-of-conflict-avoidance.
162 Joseph Grenny, quoted in Brandon West, "What GLS 2020 Taught Us About Life and Leadership," *PHOS*, 22 Aug 2020, https://phoscreative.com/articles/what-gls-2020-taught-us/.
163 "State of Business Communication in 2023."
164 Alden Mills, *Unstoppable Teams: The Four Essential Actions of High-Performance Leadership* (New York: Harper Business, 2019), 83.
165 Kevin Hall, *Aspire: Discovering Your Purpose Through the Power of Words* (New York: William Morrow, 2009), 165-166.
166 Brandon Busteed, "The Two Most Important Questions for Graduates," *Gallup*, 12 June 2015, https://news.gallup.com/opinion/gallup/183599/two-important-questions-graduates.aspx.
167 Keith E. Webb, *The Coach Model for Christian Leaders* (New York: Morgan James Publishing, 2019) 3-4.
168 "Live Your Best Life Using Your Strengths," CliftonStrengths, *Gallup*, 4 June 2024, https://www.gallup.com/cliftonstrengths/en/home.aspx.
169 "What Makes a Leader?" Leadership Practices Inventory, *The Leadership Challenge*, https://www.leadershipchallenge.com.
170 Mother Teresa, quoted by John Maxwell, *The 5 Levels of Leadership: Proven Steps to Maximize Your Potential* (New York: Center Street, 2011), 110.

ABOUT THE AUTHOR

STEPHEN BLANDINO is the lead pastor of 7 City Church, an author, blogger, leadership coach, and host of the Leader Fluent Podcast. With over thirty years of experience in local church and nonprofit leadership, Stephen is passionate about helping people engage in personal growth, develop their full leadership capacity, and produce effective, Kingdom-advancing ministry. He holds a Master's in Organizational Leadership from Regent University. Stephen lives in the Fort Worth, Texas, area with his wife Karen. They have one daughter, Ashley, a son-in-law, Dylan, and two grandsons, Elijah and Wyatt.

Contact Stephen Blandino

- stephenblandino.com
- stephenblandino
- pastorstephenblandino
- blandinostephen

RESOURCES

Check out the *Leader Fluent* Podcast with Stephen Blandino.

Each episode equips leaders to create thriving churches and organizations. Subscribe today on your favorite podcasting platform.

Study guide and Masterclass available at
insanelypracticalleadership.com

AVAIL +

TRY FOR 30 DAYS AND RECEIVE
THE SEQUENCE TO SUCCESS
BUNDLE FREE

$79 VALUE

+ BOOK
+ STUDY GUIDE
+ ONLINE COURSE
+ LIVE CLASS
+ MORE

The Art *of* Leadership

This isn't just another leadership collective...this is the next level of networking, resources, and empowerment designed specifically for leaders like you.

Whether you're an innovator in ministry, business, or your community, **AVAIL +** is designed to take you to your next level. Each one of us needs connection. Each one of us needs practical advice. Each one of us needs inspiration. **AVAIL +** is all about equipping you, so that you can turn around and equip those you lead.

THEARTOFLEADERSHIP.COM/CHAND

www.ingramcontent.com/pod-product-compliance
Lightning Source LLC
Chambersburg PA
CBHW070529090426
42735CB00013B/2921